HEROES

Brother Andrew

2006

Other Books in the Today's Heroes Series

★ TODAY'S ★
HEROES

Brother Andrew

Gregg & Deborah Shaw Lewis

Zonderkidz

Zonder**kidz**™

The children's group of Zondervan

www.zonderkidz.com

Today's Heroes: Brother Andrew
Copyright © 2002 by Open Doors International

Requests for information should be addressed to:
Grand Rapids, Michigan 49530

ISBN: 0-310-70313-1

Published in association with Yates and Yates, LLP, Literacy Agent, Orange, CA.

Photography used by permission of Open Doors
Editor: Barbara J. Scott
Interior design: Todd Sprague
Art direction: Michelle Lenger
Printed in the United States of America

02 03 04 05 06 07/❖DC/ 10 9 8 7 6 5 4 3 2 1

CONTENTS

1

SEARCHING FOR ADVENTURE

Andrew stared down at his broken wooden shoes. He had cracked his *klompen* over the head of his friend Kees. He was in trouble now.

Andrew and Kees had been playing war. But for now, their favorite game was forgotten. Like most boys living in Holland before World War II, Andrew couldn't afford more than one pair of klompen. So he expected a scolding when he took his broken shoe to his father, a blacksmith.

"Andrew, you must be more careful!" Because his father was mostly deaf, he spoke loudly.

Andrew nodded in response to his father's words, but being careful wasn't something he wanted to do. He dreamed of future adventures as a spy behind enemy lines, a secret agent caught up in sabotage and danger.

For now he had to make his own adventures. Each Sunday Andrew's family walked to church and sat near the front, where his papa could hear better. But the pew couldn't hold both of his parents, his two sisters, and all four brothers. So Andrew always let the others go in first. Then, pretending to look for an open seat on the back pews of the church, he would slip out the rear door and spend his church time playing in the fields or, in the winter, skating down frozen canals.

Just in time for the end of the service, Andrew would sneak back in. As the congregation filed out of the church, he gathered information he could use later. If someone commented, "Pastor, you made a good point about Psalm 120," that would be Andrew's ammunition. At home later, he would turn to his father and, in a very loud voice, so his father—and everyone else in the house—could hear, he would say, "Wasn't that a good point the pastor made about Psalm 120?"

No one ever seemed to notice that Andrew rarely stayed in the church service.

Among Andrew's favorite "enemies" in his adventures was a family named Whetstra. They were the first people in Witte to talk about the Germans and the possibility of a real war. No one else wanted to even think about that. Andrew thought Mr. Whetstra's ominous warnings about the Nazis were tiresome. And the Whetstras were outspoken Christians whose talk of "the Lord willing" and "God bless you" irritated Andrew.

One day Andrew walked by his neighbors' house, looked in the window, and saw Mrs. Whetstra putting a pan of cookies into her wood-burning stove. Then he caught sight of a new pane of glass, leaning against the house, waiting for Mr. Whetstra to install it. This was Andrew's chance to get the Whetstras and have an adventure doing it! He crept up to the house and got the pane of glass. Then he sneaked around back, where, like all the houses in Witte, a ladder led up to the thatched roof. Andrew climbed the ladder and quietly slid the glass over the chimney.

Andrew quickly backed down the ladder and hid across the street to watch. He didn't have to wait long. Smoke backed up into the kitchen and billowed out the window. Mrs. Whetstra screamed; Mr. Whetstra ran outside and looked up at the chimney. As Mr. Whetstra climbed the ladder to remove the pane of glass, Andrew grinned at his secret victory over his "enemies."

Andrew's family had four boys: Bastian, Ben, Andrew, and Cornelius. He also had two sisters, Geltje and Maartje. Andrew especially loved his oldest brother Bastian or Bas as everyone called him. Bas was six years older than Andrew, but he wasn't like the other children. He had never learned to talk or dress himself because he was developmentally disabled, which means he had a hard time learning. Each morning, rain or shine, Bas wandered out of their home and down the street to an elm tree. There he spent his days standing and smiling as people went by, until one of his brothers would come to lead him home for supper. People would nod back and say, sadly, "Ah, Bas." Those were the only words Bas ever learned to say, having heard them repeated so often.

Most evenings, Andrew's family would gather around the small pump organ in the parlor of their home. Bas would crawl under the keyboard and press his ear to the baseboard to listen to Papa play as many wrong notes as right ones.

From underneath the keyboard, Bas could not see Papa's fingers on the keys. But it didn't matter. After several songs, Bas would stand, and Papa would let Bas take his place on the bench. Bas couldn't read the music and often managed to get the hymnal turned upside down. But he played the songs perfectly, with such beauty and feeling, that neighbors would gather by the windows to listen.

Andrew's brother Ben shared a loft bedroom with him. Ben earned money running errands for neighbors or helping the schoolteacher with her garden. He stored the pennies he earned in a piggy bank kept in his corner of the room.

One day Andrew decided that his next adventure would be to relieve his brother of some of that hidden treasure. It took Andrew about fifteen very tense minutes to slip enough pennies from the penny bank to equal one guilder. That part had been exciting! But then Andrew realized he had a problem. A guilder was worth twenty-five cents—a lot of money for a child in the 1930s. If he took that much to the candy store to spend, the storeowner would ask where Andrew had gotten the money.

So Andrew came up with a plan. The next day he showed the money to the schoolmistress Miss Meekle, saying he had found it in the street.

"Can I keep it?" Andrew asked.

"You must take it to the police. They will tell you what to do."

Andrew hadn't counted on that. But he summoned his courage and took the money to the police station, hoping nothing would give him away.

However, the police chief seemed to believe him. He took the money, sealed it in an envelope with Andrew's name on it, and told him that if no one claimed it within a year, it would be his.

A year later Andrew claimed the money and made his trip to the candy store. But during that year, Ben had never missed his guilder. That made the episode seem less like an adventure and more like common theft.

2

NO LONGER A GAME

By the time Andrew was ten years old, more people were beginning to talk about war—not as a children's game but as a real possibility. And now everyone considered Germany a real threat.

Most families in Witte had radios in their homes and listened to news and music concerts. Occasionally, they would hear the harsh, screaming voice of Germany's ruler, Adolf Hitler, bellowing out threats. At first the people of Witte thought the little man with the big voice and the hate-filled message was almost comical.

But the people of Holland watched as Hitler took over the country of Czechoslovakia and signed a treaty with Russia. Then Germany launched its *blitzkrieg*—"lightning war"—against

Poland, overrunning that country in less than a month. The next countries to fall were Norway and Denmark. And the citizens of Witte could only hope Hitler would let Holland stay neutral.

But in Andrew's home, attention centered on another battle: the one his brother Bas was fighting with tuberculosis—a dreadful disease of the lungs. Andrew watched as Bas, coughing and coughing, lost that battle slowly over the course of several months. One day, just after his eleventh birthday, Andrew decided if Bas died, he didn't want to live either. So he made plans to catch the disease himself. Andrew watched for an opportunity to sneak in to see Bas. This was forbidden, since the tuberculosis was contagious.

Andrew waited until his mother was busy in the kitchen, then slipped into the room and kissed Bas again and again. But his ploy did not work. Two months later, Bas died, and Andrew lived on as healthy as ever.

In the following months the Dutch began to prepare for war. Hoping to slow any German invasion, Holland did something that broke the hearts of its citizens—they began to blow up their dikes. Over the course of several centuries, Holland had built walls of dirt around marshes or areas covered by the sea. Then they had pumped the water out from behind the dike, creating a polder. By World War II, thousands of people lived in and farmed this rich land reclaimed from the sea. So when the dikes were destroyed and the land flooded again, many people lost their homes.

Yet this costly strategy didn't slow the Germans. They came by air, not over the land or sea.

On Andrew's twelfth birthday, the German *Luftwaffe* (air force) bombed the small military airfield near Witte. Andrew watched the planes fly overhead and cringed at the explosions only three miles away. For the next few days everyone huddled in their homes, listening to radio reports. They heard Germans were bombing airports all over the country, that German soldiers had parachuted into Holland's major cities and captured strategic bridges, and that in one hour of assault from the *Luftwaffe*, the Germans had destroyed the entire city of Rotterdam.

Holland surrendered the next day. War was suddenly no longer a game played by children. Andrew's adventures soon became deadly serious.

Witte was a small village—too small to require Hitler's best troops. One Nazi lieutenant and a handful of older soldiers served as the Germans' occupation force in his town. But to Andrew, they were the enemy, and that was enough for him.

Andrew crept out of his home at 2:00 in the morning to begin his adventure of resistance. A small amount of sugar, pilfered from his mother's pantry and slipped into the gas tank, fouled the spark plugs and stalled the lieutenant's car.

With that success behind him, Andrew decided on a bolder move. He gathered a basketful of precious vegetables, now in short supply, and headed for the nearby town. There he exchanged them for prewar fireworks, including one gigantic cherry bomb, which he put in the bottom of his basket covered with flowers, and headed home.

That night Andrew slipped out the door and pressed himself against the side of the house as a patrol of four German soldiers made their way down the street, shining their flashlights on each building as they passed. Then he ran as fast as he could up the street, where he placed the cherry bomb in the doorway of the lieutenant's quarters. To make things more exciting, Andrew waited until the patrol was almost back before he lit the fuse. Then he ran.

"Halt!" Andrew heard the sound of a rifle bolt being drawn. He began zigging and zagging up the street on the run. When the cherry bomb exploded, the soldiers turned and looked back. That gave Andrew the chance he needed to dash across a bridge and throw himself down in a cabbage patch. There he lay for an hour while the Germans searched up and down the streets of Witte. When they finally gave up, he was able to sneak back home.

One day Andrew got caught! He had firecrackers in one hand and a match in the other when a German soldier snapped, *"Du! Komm mal her!"*

Andrew closed his hands around the firecrackers and the match. He couldn't stuff them in his pocket—that would be the first place the soldier would look.

"Hast du einen Fuerwerkskoerper explodiert?" the soldier demanded.

"Fuerwerks? Oh, no, sir!" Andrew responded. He grabbed the edges of his coat, fireworks and match still in his hands, and held his coat open for the German to search. And he did search, thoroughly, except he never bothered to look in Andrew's hands. But by the time the soldier let Andrew go, his hands had sweated so much that the firecrackers and the match would no longer light.

As exciting as Andrew's adventures against the Germans were, his mischief didn't seem to be making much difference. The Nazis took hostages in nearby towns, lined them up, and shot them. Men and boys—called *onderduikers*—went into hiding to escape being captured and taken to labor camps. Andrew's brother Ben "dove under" during the first month of the war, and his family didn't hear from him again for five years.

The new Nazi government made it a crime to own a radio. So Andrew's family hid theirs in a crawl space, where one person at a time could huddle to listen to news. And in that same crawl space, they occasionally hid people on the run from the Germans. These were Jews and, when the Dutch railroad went on strike, railway workers.

Before Andrew was fourteen years old, the Germans became desperate for laborers. German trucks would speed into town and seal the roads going in and out. German soldiers would grab any able-bodied man they found and drag him away to the labor camps. Andrew joined the other boys and men, running hunched-over across the fields, leaping over canals, and heading for the swamp. Each time they had to dive into the last canal and swim to safety, climbing out on the other side, shivering with cold.

Only the Germans had coal for heat, electricity, or food. Andrew's father still worked his garden, but the Germans often came and took the food for themselves. Andrew's family dug up the tulip bulbs in their garden and ate them like potatoes. By the end of the war, even the tulips were gone, and Andrew's mother lay dying of hunger.

Finally, in the spring of 1945, Canadians liberated the town of Witte, and Andrew raced as fast as he could to the Canadian camp five miles away. There he begged a small sackful of bread crusts to save his mother from starvation. Then he ran back home, calling "Food! Food!"

3

THE WOUNDS OF WAR

One afternoon soon after the war ended, Andrew's little sister Geltje told him Papa wanted to talk to him. So Andrew found his father weeding the cabbage patch.

As usual, Andrew had to shout to be heard. "You wanted to see me, Papa?"

His father slowly straightened up and looked at his son. "You're seventeen years old, Andrew."

"Yes, sir."

"What do you plan to do with your life?"

"I don't know, Papa."

He didn't want to take up smithing like his father. He thought that was boring.

His father simply said, "It's time for you to choose a trade, Andrew. By fall I want your decision." That was the end of the conversation.

All Andrew could think about was how badly he wanted to get away from the little town of Witte, break out of the mold, and find adventure. But his choices were limited. He'd stopped going to school in the sixth grade when the German forces had taken over the local school building.

Running was the only thing Andrew was really good at. So that afternoon, he took off across the polders. Mile after mile he ran, his thoughts taking shape as he raced barefoot along the dikes. The papers were full of stories about the Dutch East Indies now talking about declaring independence from Holland. They had been Dutch colonies for more than three centuries, and the Dutch people wanted to keep them.

That night Andrew announced to his father and the rest of the family that he already knew what he was going to do. "I'm going to join the army and go to the East Indies."

Andrew's mother, who'd seen too much of armies, gasped in surprise. "Oh, Andrew," she said, "must we always think of killing?" But his father and brothers were more supportive.

The next week Andrew borrowed his father's bicycle and pedaled to the recruitment office in Amsterdam. Before long, he was strutting back to Witte in a used and ill-fitting army uniform. He was a soldier now, determined to take the colonies back for the queen.

The only townspeople who didn't respond with applause were the Whetstras. But Mr. Whetstra made a point of calling out a greeting: "Hello there, Andrew!"

"Good morning, Mr. Whetstra!"

His neighbor didn't even seem to notice the uniform.

"I've joined up," Andrew announced. "I'm going to the East Indies."

Mr. Whetstra leaned back and carefully looked him over. "Yes, I see. So you're off for adventure. I will pray for you, Andrew. I will pray that the adventure you find will be satisfying."

Andrew thought that was a strange response. Any adventure would be more satisfying than being stuck in Witte the rest of his life.

Basic training was more difficult than he'd imagined. But Andrew loved it. For the first time in his life, he was doing something he wanted to do. And he was finally being treated like an adult.

November 22, 1946, was Andrew's last day at home. As his mother hugged him goodbye, she reached under her apron and drew out her Bible.

"Will you take this with you and read it?"

He couldn't say no to his mother. So he took the Bible and put it in his duffle bag, as far down as it would go, and forgot all about it.

Andrew's transport ship landed in Indonesia just before Christmas 1946. Along with other soldiers who qualified, Andrew was sent to a nearby island for special commando training. In an exotic tropical paradise halfway around the world from his home, the whole experience seemed like an exciting, challenging game. That is, until his unit received its first combat assignment.

One morning at dawn, Andrew and his buddies were flown to the war front to relieve a company of commandos that rumor said had lost three out of four of its men. Andrew soon realized he didn't like this adventure. It wasn't the danger that bothered him—he liked that. It was the killing. He was no longer shooting at paper targets, but real men— fathers and brothers like his own.

After fighting all day, he would lie awake in the jungle darkness, wondering *How did I get here?*

One time after three straight weeks of daily combat, Andrew's company was walking through a peaceful-looking village when one of his comrades stepped into a nest of antipersonnel mines. Such mines were a soldier's greatest fear—explosions that could result in a horrible, bloody death or leave him terribly crippled for life. So when the first explosion went off, the entire company went berserk. Without orders, without thinking, every-one started shooting. They shot everything in sight.

When they finally stopped, there wasn't a living thing left in that village. The soldiers care-fully skirted the minefield and made their way through the village they had just destroyed. At the edge of the village, Andrew stumbled on a young Indonesian mother who lay on the ground in a pool of her blood, a baby boy at her breast. The same bullet had killed both. Had it been his bullet? Andrew would never know. But the question would haunt him for the rest of his life.

After that, Andrew acted like he didn't care whether he lived or died. He became famous for reckless, crazy bravado on the battlefield. He bought a bright yellow straw hat and wore it into battle as a dare. "Here I am! Shoot me!" it said.

Gradually, Andrew attracted a whole group of guys who reacted to the war as he did. They posted their motto on the camp bulletin board: "Get smart—lose your mind!" When they fought, they fought like madmen. When they drank, they would get falling-down drunk.

Andrew would wake up from his drunken binges wondering why he was acting so recklessly. He never could answer the question. He wrote home about his feelings of confusion. Everyone who wrote back said, "You're fighting for your country, Andrew. So the rest doesn't matter." Still, he couldn't shake the feelings of guilt. They seemed to wrap around him like a chain. And nothing he did—drinking, fighting, writing letters, or reading the replies—eased their stranglehold.

One day Andrew was on leave in the city of Jakarta. As he walked through the bazaar, a little gibbon sitting on top of a pole eating fruit leaped onto his shoulder and handed him a section of orange. When Andrew laughed, an Indonesian salesman came running. "The monkey likes you."

Andrew laughed again. "How much?"

They quickly settled on a price, and Andrew had a new pet and a new friend. He hadn't had the monkey very long before he noticed what seemed like a welt around his middle. He put the little fella down on the bed and told him to hold still while he carefully pulled back the hair to see what the problem was. Evidently, when the young gibbon had been captured, someone had tied a wire around his waist and never taken it off. As the monkey grew, the wire became embedded in his flesh and was causing terrible pain.

That evening, Andrew took his razor and shaved the hair around the monkey's middle. The uncovered welt looked red and angry. Then Andrew cut gently into the tender skin until he exposed the wire. Amazingly, the gibbon lay still until Andrew finally pulled the wire off. Then he jumped up, turned a cartwheel, leaped onto Andrew's shoulder, and began pulling his hair.

After that, Andrew and the gibbon were inseparable. When Andrew wasn't on duty, he'd take the gibbon with him on long runs through the nearby rainforests. The monkey loped along behind Andrew until he got tired. Then he'd sprint forward, leap up, and grab onto Andrew's shorts until Andrew would swing him up on his shoulder. Together they would run for ten or fifteen miles before Andrew would fling himself down on the ground to rest. Usually, there would be monkeys in the trees overhead, and the gibbon would race into the treetops and chatter with his new friends until Andrew awakened and headed back. Then there'd be a shriek overhead, a rustle of leaves, and a thud as the little monkey leaped down on Andrew's shoulder for the ride back to the base.

One day when Andrew carried him back into camp laughing and tired, he found a letter from home. His mother had died. Andrew knew he was going to cry, so he gave the gibbon some water and, while he was drinking, slipped away from camp to be alone. He ran until his side ached, thinking how much he was going to miss his mother.

With news of a major new drive against the enemy, Andrew recruited a buddy with a jeep to drive him and his pet into the jungle. As they rode, he tried to explain to the monkey why he could no longer keep him. When they stopped, he put his little friend on the ground. The gibbon just sat sadly and watched while the jeep pulled out of sight. As it turned out, it was a good thing Andrew let the monkey go when he did.

During their next offensive, Andrew and his company walked into an ambush. Suddenly, they were taking fire from three sides. As he turned and raced back in retreat, Andrew fell. His right combat boot had two holes in it, and blood was pouring out of both holes.

"I'm hit," he called. Another soldier rolled him into a ditch. Finally, two medics arrived and put him on a stretcher. Andrew was still wearing his yellow hat and refused to take it off.

At the hospital, Andrew heard the doctors discussing amputation before they operated for two and a half hours to sew up his foot. A nurse asked him to take off his hat. Again he refused.

"Don't you know what that is?" one of the doctors asked. "That's the unit's symbol. These are the boys who got smart and lost their minds."

But Andrew had even failed at that. He hadn't managed to get his brains blown out—just a foot.

He had come to Indonesia in search of excitement and honor. In the end, angry at everyone and everything, he'd resigned himself to a death of glory . . . or foolishness. He didn't care which.

But instead, he was going home alive—as a cripple. His adventure had been a total failure.

4

GOING HOME

One day as he thrashed restlessly around in his narrow hospital bed, his right leg in a heavy plaster cast, Andrew flung out his arm, and his hand fell on a book. One of his buddies had found his mother's little Bible in Andrew's duffel bag and left it out on the bedside table.

Andrew hadn't opened it in the years since his mother had given it to him. But now Andrew slowly flipped through the pages from back to front until he came to Genesis 1:1.

Andrew began to read, skipping some passages but following the basic story with more interest than he'd ever had in church or in school. Days later when he finally got to the New Testament, Andrew read straight through the Gospels. Could this really be true? Did God really love him so much that he sent his Son to die for Andrew's sins? It sounded too wonderful to be true.

As the months passed and his cast was removed bit by bit, Andrew spent a lot of time staring at his ugly, shriveled leg and remembering what it was like to run like the wind over the polders back home. He knew the joy of running would never be his again. And he resented it.

When his wound healed enough that he could get out of bed and hobble around a bit, Andrew left the hospital every evening and limped painfully to the nearest pub. He would drink until he no longer felt or even remembered his pain and anger.

The day before he was finally shipped home, Andrew's favorite nurse nun, Sister Patrice, came and sat in a chair next to his bed. "I have a story to tell you, Andrew," she said. "Do you know how natives catch monkeys in the jungle?"

He smiled and thought of his pet monkey. "No. Tell me."

"Well, the natives know a monkey never wants to let go of something he thinks he wants. So they take a coconut and make a hole in one end just large enough for a monkey to slip his paw through. Then they drop a pebble into the hole and hide in the bushes with a net. Sooner or later, a curious little fellow will come along, pick up that coconut, and hear the pebble rattling inside.

He will try to look in the hole. Then he will slip his paw in and feel around until he gets hold of that pebble. But when he tries to bring it out, he finds that he can't get his paw out of the hole without letting go of his prize. Then the natives pounce on him with the net. The monkey can't escape because he won't let go of the pebble and free his hand from the coconut."

The sister looked Andrew right in the eye. "Are you holding on to something that's keeping you from being free, Andrew?"

He knew what she meant. But Andrew didn't want to admit it to her or to himself.

The next day was his twenty-first birthday. It was also the day the hospital ship sailed for home. So he invited all the survivors of the company he'd come to Indonesia with three years earlier to his going-away party. Counting Andrew, eight remained. And they all got rip-roaring drunk.

When Andrew arrived back in Witte, he limped slowly toward the house. His sister Geltje shouted, "Andrew!" and came running across the little bridge to give him a big welcome-home hug. Maartje kissed him, and everyone else crowded around. Then his papa came shuffling around the house with tears in his eyes, shouting, "Andrew, boy! Good to have you home!"

His sisters showed him where his mother had been buried. Later that evening, Andrew borrowed his father's bicycle, threw his bad leg over the seat, and pushed himself—half-riding and half-walking—back to the cemetery.

Sitting on the ground next to the grave, he said softly, "I'm back, Mama." He spoke as if she were right there. "I did read your Bible, Mama. Not at first, but I did read it."

After a long silence, he spoke again. "What am I going to do now, Mama? I can't walk a hundred yards without the pain making me stop. I'm no good at smithing. I feel so useless, Mama. And guilty. Guilty for the life I led out there. Answer me, Mama." No answer. Finally he wheeled himself home, where he slowly, painfully climbed the ladder to the loft and slept in his old bed under the eaves.

The next morning, Andrew took his cane and began a long walk through the village. Mr. Whetstra invited him in for coffee. "Did you find the adventure you were looking for, Andrew?"

"Not really." Andrew stared at the floor.

"Well, then," Mr. Whetstra said, "we'll just have to keep praying."

"Sure. I'm a real natural for adventure now," Andrew responded bitterly. "I'll limp right out to meet it when it comes!" But as soon as he said it, he was embarrassed at his outburst.

When he left the Whetstras, Andrew visited another old friend, Kees, at home in his room with a stack of books. Picking up one of the volumes, Andrew noticed it was about God. "What's this?"

"I've decided what I'm going to do with my life," Kees explained.

"You're lucky, then," Andrew told his friend. "What is it?"

"I want to go into the ministry," Kees said.

That bothered Andrew so much he left as soon as he could.

After visiting his family for a few days, Andrew went to a veterans' hospital at Doorn for more rehabilitation. He hated the therapy and grew even more discouraged by his lack of progress.

Months passed. One morning Andrew and several fellow patients were sitting on their beds reading or writing letters when a nurse came in to announce that a visitor had arrived. He didn't look up until he heard the boys begin to whistle.

"I won't take much of your time," a beautiful blonde girl began. "I just wanted to invite you to our tent meeting tonight. The bus will leave at 7:00 P.M., and I hope you can all come."

The boys clapped and cheered, "Encore! Encore!" as she retreated out of the room. But they were all in line for the bus right on time, and Andrew was right in front. The soldiers finished off a bottle of liquor on the way to the service and then talked and laughed so loudly during a prayer that they disrupted the entire program. The man abruptly ended his prayer and called on the choir to sing "Let My People Go."

Even after the service ended and the veterans climbed aboard the bus that would take them back to the hospital, the words of the song kept echoing in Andrew's mind: "Let them go . . . let me go."

The next day he picked up his Bible for the first time since he returned to Holland. He began to read. This time his mother's book read like a real adventure novel. Andrew devoured it.

When he went home again for a long weekend, Andrew spent so much time lying in his room reading the Bible that his family began to worry about him. And when he began showing up at church every time the doors opened, the whole town seemed to take notice.

Andrew was finally mustered out of the army a few months later and bought a new bike with his separation pay. He soon learned to pedal with his good leg and coast with the bad.

Now he could attend church in neighboring towns as well. He found some church service to attend every night of the week.

His sister Maartje finally confronted him about his constant Bible reading and about going to church every night. "It isn't natural! What's happened to you, Andrew?"

He smiled and told her, "I wish I knew."

Andrew began spending a lot more time talking with Kees, with his old schoolteacher Miss Meekle, and with the Whetstras.

Then late one dark winter night in 1950, lying in bed and listening to sleet blowing across the polders, it was as if he could hear voices in the wind. He heard Sister Patrice saying, "The monkey will never let go . . ." He also heard singing under a tent, "Let my people go . . ."

What am I hanging on to? he asked himself. *What's hanging onto me?*

With the wind howling and everyone else in the house asleep, Andrew lay on his back, staring at the ceiling. Suddenly, he let go—of his bitterness, his discouragement, his dreams, everything.

He later explained it by saying, "With a new note in the wind yelling at me not to be a fool, I turned myself over to God—lock, stock, and adventure. There wasn't much faith in my prayer. I just said, 'Lord, if you will show me the way, I will follow you. Amen.' It was as simple as that."

Little did Andrew know that prayer would be the beginning of a whole new adventure—greater than any he'd ever experienced or even imagined—that would continue for the rest of his life.

5

WHOLE AT LAST

Andrew awakened the next morning so happy he had to tell someone what had happened. His family was already worried about him. So he went to visit the Whetstras, who understood right away. Philip Whetstra shouted, "Praise the Lord!" He acted as if what Andrew had done wasn't strange at all; he called it being "born again." While Andrew wasn't sure what that meant, the Whetstras' excitement warmed his heart and gave him the idea that what he'd done was important.

His friend Kees also seemed to understand. He told Andrew he'd be interested to see what changes might come about as a result.

A few weeks later Andrew and Kees traveled to Amsterdam to hear a well-known Dutch preacher. Near the end of the sermon, Pastor Arne Donker suddenly stopped and said, "Friends, I've had a feeling all night that someone here is being called by God to become a missionary."

Andrew began to feel uncomfortable. "I hate this sort of thing," Kees whispered. "Let's leave." But as they edged toward the aisle, people turned to look. So they quickly sat back down.

"God knows who it is," Rev. Donker said. "I think it's probably a young man."

People all over the hall looked around. Suddenly, without ever deciding to move, almost as if something or someone had plucked them out of their seats, Andrew and Kees were on their feet.

"Splendid," the preacher exclaimed. "Will you boys come forward?" After he prayed over them, the evangelist asked them to stay and talk after the service. So when the hall finally emptied, he asked their names. Then he asked, "Are you boys ready for your first assignment?"

Before they could answer he asked where they were from. "Both from Witte? Excellent! I want you to go back to Witte and hold an open-air meeting in the middle of town. You'll be following a biblical pattern," he assured them. "Jesus told his disciples to spread the good news—beginning at Jerusalem in their own hometown."

Rev. Donker must have seen the shocked looks on the boys' faces, because he quickly assured them, "Oh, I'll be with you, boys! Nothing to be alarmed about. It's all in getting used to it. I'll speak first . . . So we have a date then?"

Andrew wanted to scream no! But when he opened his mouth, he heard himself say yes instead.

When Saturday came, it seemed everyone in town showed up. Andrew saw some familiar faces grinning at him in amusement. A few people were laughing out loud. The Whetstras and Miss Meekle smiled and nodded encouragement.

Andrew felt so nervous he didn't hear a thing Rev. Donker or Kees said. Then it was his turn. He forgot what he had planned to say. So he told how he'd come home from Indonesia feeling dirty and guilty. How he'd carried around the burden of what he was and what he wanted out of life until one night during a storm he had "laid it all down." He went on to tell how free he'd felt ever since—"free, that is, until Rev. Donker trapped me into saying I wanted to become a missionary. But you know, I might surprise him at that."

What Rev. Donker said about first being a missionary at home made sense to Andrew. He decided to get a job around Witte and find out if he was cut out to be a missionary after all.

The largest industry in the area was Ringer's chocolate factory in the nearby town of Alkmaar. Andrew strode through the door of their hiring office as briskly as he could.

The personnel director gave Andrew a job. He was to count the boxes coming off the end of an assembly line and wheel them to the shipping room. A young boy led him out to the assembly room, where two hundred girls worked along a dozen conveyor belts. He left Andrew after announcing, "Girls, this is Andrew. Have fun!"

Andrew turned red with embarrassment at the chorus of whistles and catcalls greeting his introduction. Even his years in the army hadn't prepared him for the kind of foul language and dirty jokes he heard that morning—most aimed at him. The ringleader seemed to be a loud-mouthed girl named Greetje. She gave him such a hard time that Andrew could hardly wait to fill his cart and escape for a few minutes to the peace and quiet of the all-male shipping room.

But too soon his cart was unloaded, and he had to return to the assembly room. *This may be a mission field, Lord,* he thought as he took his receipt for the first cart of boxes to the time-keeper's window. *But it's not my mission field.*

Andrew suddenly stopped. Smiling at him through the glass partition of the timekeeper's booth were the softest, warmest eyes he'd ever seen. Green. No, brown. They seemed to change colors even as he stared. The girl they belonged to was young and blonde and slender—a teenager.

Yet she had the most responsible job on the floor—handling receipts and keeping records.

As Andrew handed over his paperwork, the girl's smile became a laugh. She told him not to mind the other girls. "They give this treatment to every newcomer. In a day or two, they'll be picking on someone else." As she handed Andrew his receipt, he continued to stare. He was sure he'd seen her before. But he didn't tell her that. He just headed back out on the floor for another load.

By the end of that first long day, Andrew's ankle throbbed so much he couldn't help limping. Greetje noticed right away. "What's wrong, Andrew?" she called. "You fall out of bed?"

"East Indies," he replied, hoping that would shut her up. It did just the opposite.

"Oh, girls—we have a war hero here." The next several days, they teased him about that.

For the first month, the only good thing about the job was the smiling eyes in the glass booth. He stopped there every chance he got. And he felt more and more certain that he knew the girl from somewhere. Finally, he worked up the courage to tell her, "I'm worried about you. You're too young and too pretty to be working with this crowd."

She laughed out loud. "Why, Grampa!" she told him. "What old-fashioned ideas you have." Then she leaned toward him and lowered her voice. "They aren't a bad crowd really. Most of them just need friends." She paused, uncertain about whether to go on. Then she said softly, "You see, I'm a Christian. That's why I came to work here."

Suddenly, Andrew remembered where he'd seen her. She was the girl who'd come to the veterans' hospital. The one who invited the patients to that tent meeting where they'd all behaved so badly.

Andrew quickly told her his story. He explained that he had turned his life over to God and come to work at Ringer's for much the same reason she had. He learned his fellow missionary's name was Corrie van Dam. From that day on, Andrew and Corrie were a team. They invited some of their fellow workers to go with them to a nearby conference center, where an evangelist was holding Christian youth rallies every weekend.

One day Greetje started teasing one of the other workers whom Andrew and Corrie had befriended. Amy was blind and worked on the same conveyor belt with Greetje. She was almost in tears when Andrew shouted across the room: "Greetje, shut up! And shut up for good!"

The assembly room fell silent. Greetje's mouth dropped open. Andrew surprised himself even more by adding: "And Greetje, the bus leaves for the conference center at 9:00 A.M. on Saturday. I want you to be on board."

Andrew expected her to make some kind of joke, but Greetje simply said, "All right." She surprised him again on Saturday when she boarded the bus. During the services, she made wisecracks as young people on the platform told how God was making a difference in their lives. In between sessions, she read a trashy romance novel.

Sunday afternoon, when the bus returned to the Akmaar depot where he had left his bike, Andrew offered Greetje a ride home to save her bus fare. He figured the ride would give him a chance to convince her of her need for God. Instead, God seemed to be telling him, *Not one word about religion. Just admire the scenery*. So that's what he did.

The next day at lunch, Greetje plopped her tray down beside Andrew's. She told him she'd expected him to preach at her on the ride home the day before. "When you didn't, I began to wonder, 'Does Andrew think I've gone so far that there's no turning back?' Then I began to wonder if maybe I *had* gone too far. Would God still listen if I said I was sorry? Would he let me start all over again, like those kids at the conference claimed? Anyhow, I asked him to. It was a pretty funny prayer, but I meant it. And, Andrew, I began to cry. I cried almost all night. But this morning I feel great."

Greetje was a new person and still a leader! She stopped telling dirty stories, so most of the other girls stopped too. When Andrew and Corrie started a company prayer meeting, Greetje took charge of attendance. Soon the whole factory seemed like a different place.

One day the owner of the company, asked to see Andrew. He told him that recent testing done by the company revealed Andrew had an exceptional IQ. Andrew wasn't sure what that meant, but he figured it was good because Mr. Ringer smiled and said whatever job Andrew saw that interested him, he could train for.

Andrew told Mr. Ringer he already knew what he wanted to do. "I want to help other people decide what jobs they are suited for." In return for the training, Andrew agreed to stay on at Ringer's for at least two more years. But even though he enjoyed his new job, as time went on, he became more and more convinced that God was calling him to be a missionary somewhere else.

Andrew was discouraged when he learned that church missionaries had to go to seminary. That meant making up for the schooling he missed during the war, then going on to study theology in seminary. It would take twelve years. He was already twenty-four. He'd be thirty-six before he could even graduate from seminary and begin working as a missionary. Surely there was a quicker way!

A friend told him about the Worldwide Evangelization Crusade (WEC)—a British group training lay people to take the gospel into parts of the world where churches had not yet sent missionaries. They had a two-year training school.

After talking to a WEC official, Andrew told his friend Kees what he'd learned. Kees applied and was accepted at once. Soon he was writing letters home, telling Andrew all about what he was learning at WEC's school in Glasgow, Scotland.

Even after he'd completed the two years that he'd promised Mr. Ringer, Andrew hung back. He told himself he didn't have the formal training Kees did. And though he hid it from others fairly well, he still had a crippled ankle. He couldn't even walk a city block without terrible pain. Maybe being a missionary was just a foolish dream.

One Sunday afternoon in September 1952, Andrew went out on the polders, where he could pray out loud without being embarrassed. He sat on the edge of a canal and began to talk to God as if he were right there beside him. He determined to pray until he had an answer. He prayed into the evening. Still he hadn't found God's plan for his life.

"What is it, Lord?" he wanted to know. "What am I holding back?"

Finally he had his answer. His yes to God had always been a "Yes, but ... Yes, but I'm not educated. Yes, but I've got this crippled foot."

So Andrew said yes in a different way. No buts. "I'll go, Lord," he said to God, "whatever route you want me to take. If it's through seminary, the WEC training school, or continuing to work at Ringer's. Whenever, wherever, however you want me, I'll go. I'll begin this minute, Lord, as I stand up from this place, and I take my first step forward. It will be a step of complete confidence in you. I'll call it 'The Step of Yes.'"

Andrew stood up, and as he took that first stride, he felt a painful twisting in his injured leg. He thought he'd sprained his crippled ankle. But when he gingerly put his foot on the ground again, he could stand on it. What had happened? Slowly he began to walk home. As he walked he recalled these words: "Going they were healed." He couldn't remember exactly where the words came from. Then it hit him—in the story of Jesus and the ten lepers, *on their way* to do what Jesus had commanded them to do, a miracle happened. "And as they went, they were [healed]" (Luke 17:12). *Could that be what's happening to me?*

That night he walked to church service in a village about four miles away without any pain. The next morning at the chocolate factory, his ankle began to itch. As he rubbed the old scar, two stitches came through the skin. By the end of the week, the incision that had never healed properly completely closed.

The next week, Andrew applied to the WEC school in Scotland.

THE CALL
BECOMES CLEAR

In the fall of 1953 Andrew hurried off to Scotland to begin a two-year adventure in learning. Learning to speak English wasn't easy. But since all his professors taught their classes in that language, he had to pick it up quickly.

His friend Kees introduced him around and helped him get off to a good start. Andrew loved it.

The first semester sped by. Mornings were spent taking courses like those taught in any seminary—classes in theology, preaching, world religion, and linguistics. In the afternoons, the students learned other practical skills—plumbing, carpentry, bricklaying, first aid, tropical hygiene, motor repair, how to build huts out of palm fronds, and how to make mud containers that would hold water. They also took turns doing chores around the school.

But the most important thing Andrew learned was to trust God to take care of him. That lesson hit home one day when Andrew was worrying about how he would pay for his second semester. Andrew remembered that when he worked in the chocolate factory, he trusted Mr. Ringer to pay him what he was due and on time. *If an ordinary factory worker can be financially secure,* he told himself, *why shouldn't one of God's workers?*

That night he prayed, "Lord, I need to know if I can trust you in practical things. Thank you for letting me earn the fees for the first semester. I ask you now to supply the rest of the money I need. If I have to be so much as a day late in paying, I shall know I am supposed to go back to Ringer's."

God honored that prayer, sometimes in surprising ways. The Whetstras sent enough money to pay for his second semester. It came just in time, without him ever mentioning fees to anyone.

In the spring of 1955, Andrew's two years of training were almost over. Still he didn't know for sure where he was going to go as a missionary.

But one week before his graduation, something happened that changed Andrew's life forever. He went down into the dorm basement to get his suitcase, and there on top of an old cardboard box in that dark and dusty cellar was a magazine. A beautiful publication, printed on expensive, glossy paper, it contained big, full-color pictures of thousands of young people parading in the streets of Peking, Warsaw, and Prague. Nowhere did the word *communist* appear. But this was clearly a communist youth magazine full of talk about "a better world" and "a bright tomorrow."

In the back was an announcement about a youth festival planned for Warsaw that coming July. Everyone was invited. Andrew carried the magazine back to his room and sent a letter to the Warsaw address listed in the magazine. He wrote that he was training to be a Christian missionary and would like to come to the festival to exchange ideas. He would tell them about Christ, and they could tell him about communism. Would they be willing for him to come?

Soon Andrew received a response. Certainly they wanted him to come. Since he was a student, they would give him reduced rates on a special train leaving for Warsaw from Amsterdam.

After graduation, Andrew returned to Witte to visit his family and friends. He went to see Mr. Ringer at the factory and his old teacher Miss Meekle, who was amazed by his English. When he stopped in to see the Whetstras, he learned their flower-export business had grown so much that they were moving to Amsterdam.

Hundreds of young people boarded the train to Warsaw on July 15, 1955. Andrew carried a heavy suitcase with a few clothes and dozens of copies of a booklet entitled "The Way of Salvation" printed in various European languages.

In Warsaw, his hotel turned out to be a school building converted into a temporary dormitory. Tens of thousands of young people had come to the conference from all over the world, and many of them stayed there.

Andrew had read Dutch newspaper articles about church leaders in communist countries being persecuted and thrown into prison. The communists claimed to allow freedom of religion. People quit going to church, they said, because God was nothing more than an out-of-date superstition and the communist system was providing them with a better way. The truth was that the authorities often made life difficult for believers.

When Sunday came, instead of going to his conference, Andrew slipped away and waved down a taxi. Since the only thing Andrew knew how to say in Polish was "good day," he asked the driver in German to take him to a church. Then he tried English. Nothing. Then Andrew folded his hands as if praying and then opened them as if he were reading a book. The driver smiled and nodded. Minutes later the taxi stopped in front of a building with two spires. Andrew walked into his first church service behind the Iron Curtain (which is what Westerners called the communist countries of Eastern Europe).

He was surprised to see that the church was three-quarters full. The singing was enthusiastic, and the minister kept referring to his Bible throughout the sermon. After the service, the minister welcomed him in English. Andrew had many questions. Yes, they could worship openly if they didn't discuss political issues in church. Yes, some members of his congregation were members of the communist party. "Of course, it's a compromise," the minister shrugged. "But what can you do?"

A man asked what kind of church Andrew attended at home. When he said "Baptist," the fellow wrote down the address of a Baptist church and said, "There's a service tonight."

The meeting had already begun when Andrew arrived at the Baptist church that evening. There was a smaller, older crowd with fewer well-dressed people than he'd seen that morning. Even though he tried to slip in without attracting attention, someone noticed and passed the word to the minister that a foreigner was visiting. Andrew was immediately invited to the platform to speak.

"Anyone speak German or English?" he asked.

One woman in the congregation who spoke German came to the front. As she translated into Polish, Andrew preached his first sermon in a communist country. At the end of his short talk, the pastor said something Andrew would never forget. "We want to thank you for *being* here. Even if you had not said a word, just seeing you would have meant so much. We feel at times like we are all alone in our struggle."

In Warsaw, Andrew passed out his booklets to people on the street and visited a Bible store. The owner said Poles could still buy Bibles, but they were so rare in Russia, a smuggler with ten Bibles could make enough profit to buy a motorcycle.

His last morning in Warsaw, Andrew rose and went out at sunrise. He found a bench along a wide avenue and sat down with his pocket-sized New Testament on his lap. He intended to use the time to pray for every person he'd met on his trip. On three Sundays, he'd visited Presbyterian, Baptist, Roman Catholic, Orthodox, Reformed, and Methodist churches. Five times he'd been asked to speak. He pictured the faces of people he'd met, and he prayed for each one of them.

As he prayed, he heard military music and the sound of voices singing. Nearer it came. Then he saw them—thousands of his fellow delegates to the youth conference, marching in the final parade. They marched right past his bench.

The communist young people were ready to preach their belief that there was no God. They were ready to spread the word that man should be his own master and the future was his to take. What an impressive sight! The strength of communism had never seemed so overwhelming. What could the world do—what could he do—to counter such a powerful force?

The Bible in Andrew's lap laid open, pages ruffling in the breeze. He put his hand down to hold them and found himself looking at the book of Revelation. The verse at his fingertips, as if he were pointing to it read, "Wake up! Strengthen what remains and is about to die" (Revelation 3:2).

Sudden tears blurred the words. Could the Lord be speaking to him? Was he telling Andrew his life work was behind the Iron Curtain trying to strengthen what was left of his church?

Ridiculous! he thought. *How could I do that?* As far as he knew there wasn't a single missionary working in any of the communist countries of Eastern Europe. *What could I, one person, without any funds or organization, possibly do to make a difference behind the Iron Curtain?*

But Andrew was about to find out.

7

GREETINGS
FROM THE LORD

When Andrew climbed off the train in Amsterdam, his nearly empty suitcase felt as light as his step. Anxious as he was to get to Witte, he stopped to visit the Whetstras. Parked in front of their brick home on a tree-lined street was a shiny, light blue Volkswagen Beetle. Andrew set his suitcase on the sidewalk and tried the door. "What do you think of her, son?"

Andrew turned to find his old neighbor grinning at him. "Come on," Mr. Whetstra said, and gave him a quick spin around the waterfront.

"So much for showing off," he finally said. "You must tell us about your visit to Poland, Andrew."

For the rest of the afternoon, Andrew told his old friends about his trip. And the Bible verse he had been given. "But I don't understand it completely. It says I am to strengthen that which remains and is at the point of death. How would I strengthen anything?" he asked his old friends. "What kind of strength do I have?"

Mr. Whetstra shook his head in agreement. But Mrs. Whetstra understood. "No strength at all!" she declared with a smile. "And don't you know that it is just when we are weakest that God can use us most? Suppose now it wasn't you at all, but the Holy Spirit who had plans behind the Iron Curtain. You talk about strength . . ."

Within days of his return to Witte, invitations to speak began to arrive. Churches, civic clubs, and schools all wanted to know about life behind the Iron Curtain. A group of communists came to hear him speak at a church in Haarlem. Andrew recognized some who'd been on the trip with him. Afterward, a woman who had been the leader of the Dutch delegation in Warsaw walked up and said, "I didn't like your talk."

"I didn't think you would," Andrew told her.

"You told only part of the story," she complained. "Obviously, you haven't seen enough. You need to visit more countries, meet more leaders. And that's what I've come to suggest."

Andrew couldn't believe what she said next. "I'm in charge of selecting a group of fifteen people from Holland to take a four-week trip to Czechoslovakia. We'll have students and professors and people in communications. We'd like someone from the churches. Will you come?"

Andrew sent up a quick prayer: *If you want me to go, Lord, you'll have to supply the means.* He thanked the woman. "But I could never afford such a trip," he told her. "I'm sorry."

The woman just stood and stared at him. "Well," she finally said, "we can work that out."

"What do you mean?" Andrew asked.

"For you, there will be no charge."

Andrew's second trip behind the Iron Curtain seemed a lot like his visit to Poland, except his tour group was much smaller this time. That made it much more difficult to sneak off by himself.

He'd heard it was difficult to get Bibles into Czechoslovakia, so he talked his tour guide into taking him to a Christian bookseller in the city. The store had music, stationery, statues, and crosses, but no Bibles. When he asked the clerk to see a Bible, she told him they were out of stock.

"Ma'am," Andrew told her, "I have come all the way from Holland to see how the church is faring in Czechoslovakia. Are you telling me that I can walk into the largest religious bookstore in the country and I won't be able to buy a single Bible?"

The flustered woman disappeared into the back of the store. Andrew could hear an excited discussion taking place. A few minutes later the manager came out carrying one Bible.

He told Andrew that the reason Bibles were so scarce was because the government was sponsoring a new translation. "Until that comes out, new Bibles just aren't being printed." What he didn't say was that the government had been promising this new Bible translation for years. They never seemed to get around to printing it.

Andrew's time in Czechoslovakia was coming to an end. Still he hadn't been able to get away from his group to meet any Christians. The group's last day in Prague looked like it would be the same—a grand tour of a model community, a big final dinner, a press conference, and official goodbyes. But it was also Sunday, his last chance to attend worship without his official escort.

Andrew had planned his escape for days. He'd noticed that a broken spring kept the rear door of the tour bus from completely closing. So as the bus pulled away from the hotel that day, Andrew sat in the very back. When the guide called everyone's attention to a bronze sculpture up ahead, he saw his chance and slipped out the opening.

Half an hour later, he was standing in the vestibule of a church he'd spotted on a tour a few days earlier. Andrew slipped into a back seat to watch the congregation file in. Several people brought their hymnals, but very few had Bibles. And many people carried loose-leaf notebooks.

When the service began, everyone with a hymnal held it high so all those around them could read off the same page. People did the same with their notebooks, and Andrew saw that in the notebooks were copied, note-by-note and word-by-word, the congregations favorite hymns. The same thing happened when the minister read the Scripture. Those with Bibles held their books high so people around them could see.

After the service, Andrew introduced himself to the minister, who was overwhelmed to hear that someone had come from Holland to meet with Christians in his country. He confided that things were very difficult for Christians in Czechoslovakia. Only students who supported the government were allowed to attend seminary to be trained as ministers. Each sermon had to be written out ahead of time and approved by the authorities. Those who didn't abide by the new regulations could be thrown into prison.

It was time for the church's second service. "Would you speak to us?" the minister asked.

"Can I really preach here?"

"I did not say 'preach,'" the minister told him. "We must be careful here. But you could bring us greetings from Holland. And," he smiled, "if you wanted to, you could also bring us greetings from the Lord."

So with a medical student as his interpreter, Andrew did just as the minister suggested. His greetings from Christians in Holland took a couple of minutes. His greetings from the Lord Jesus Christ took half an hour.

It went so well that Andrew's interpreter suggested they try the same thing in another church. Before the day was over they had visited five different congregations, and Andrew preached (or "brought greetings from the Lord") to four of them.

At the last church, a number of young people crowded around him after the service. They wanted to know if Christians in Holland could get good jobs. Were they reported to the government for going to church? Could they attend church and still get into a good university?

These were problems faced by the Christians in Czechoslovakia. They paid a serious price for their beliefs. "And that," the interpreter told him, "is why they want you to have this." He took a box from one of the young men and handed it to Andrew. "Take this back to Holland with you, and when people ask you about it, tell them about us and remind them that we are part of Christ's body too. Tell them that we are in pain."

Andrew opened the box to find a small silver lapel pin in the shape of a tiny cup. He'd noticed several of the young people wearing them and wondered what they were. "This is the symbol of the church in Czechoslovakia," they told him. "We call it the Cup of Suffering."

When Andrew said goodbye to his new friends, he knew he'd remember that day forever. But his immediate problem was finding the tour group he'd left that morning.

No one at his hotel knew where his delegation's farewell dinner was being held. So Andrew walked to a restaurant where the group had eaten several times. The owner hadn't seen them, so Andrew ordered a sandwich. He'd just taken his first bite when his very angry tour guide stormed in. "Where have you been?" she demanded to know. "We called every hospital, every police station. Finally we called the morgue. Unfortunately, you were not there either!"

"Oh," Andrew replied as innocently and sincerely as he could. "I got separated from the group. So I walked around the city. I really am sorry for any trouble I've caused you."

The woman was still furious. "I want to tell you officially, sir, that you are no longer welcome in this country. Should you attempt to enter Czechoslovakia again, you will discover as much!"

Andrew was to find out later that what she said was very true.

8

ANDREW LEARNS
TO DRIVE

The next few months were frustrating for Andrew. Convinced that God wanted him to be a missionary behind the Iron Curtain, he inquired about making return trips to Poland and Czechoslovakia and other communist countries. He filled out applications, questionnaires, and forms in triplicate. But he never received a visa.

While he waited, he wrote articles about his travel experiences for a small Dutch magazine. Though he never mentioned a word about needing funds in his articles, people who read them began sending him a few guilders at a time. Just enough to replace an old jacket, purchase and send a Czech Bible to the medical student who'd translated for him, and help his family with living expenses while he was in Witte.

One day he received a letter from another reader who led a prayer group in the village of Amersfoort. It said the Holy Spirit had instructed them to invite Andrew to meet with them.

So Andrew went. He found a group of about a dozen men and women who met regularly for prayer in the home of a dike builder named Karl de Graaf. Andrew greatly enjoyed his time there with some of the godliest people he had ever met.

Several days later he was working on another magazine article when his sister Geltje called him, "There's someone to see you, Andrew." There on his front stoop was Karl de Graaf.

"Do you know how to drive an automobile, Andrew?" he asked. "Because during our prayers last night, we had a word from the Lord about you. It's important you be able to drive."

"Whatever on earth for?" Andrew almost laughed at the absurd idea. "I'll never be able to afford a car. That's for sure."

"Andrew," the dike builder said, "I'm not arguing the logic. I'm just passing on the message."

The whole idea seemed so farfetched that Andrew did nothing about it. But Mr. de Graaf came back a week later to ask, "Have you started driving lessons, Andrew?"

"Well, not exactly . . ."

"Haven't you learned yet how important it is to obey God? I suppose I'm going to have to teach you myself. Hop in."

That afternoon, Andrew sat behind the wheel of a car for the first time. Mr. de Graaf returned every week until Andrew took and passed his driver's test. He didn't understand how or why he had a license to drive an automobile when he no longer even owned a bicycle. "That's the exciting thing about obedience," Mr. de Graaf told him. "Finding out later what God had in mind."

In the fall of 1956, the people of Hungary rose up against their communist government. Russia sent tanks and soldiers to put down the revolt and help the communists regain control. Many innocent people died, and thousands of refugees flooded into the West—first from Hungary, but also from other communist-ruled countries. These refugees were herded into huge camps near the borders of Austria and West Germany. Conditions were terrible. Many families had fled with nothing more than the clothes on their backs.

Andrew volunteered to go with a group of Dutch relief workers to help in the camps. If he couldn't get to the people behind the Iron Curtain, he would help those who'd made it out. He distributed relief supplies, tried to help reunite families that had gotten separated, wrote letters, filled out visa applications, and did whatever else he could to help. He also held prayer services and conducted Bible classes. Most of the people who attended had never heard the Good News of Jesus.

Andrew was in a West Berlin refugee camp when the telegram came telling him his papa had died. He caught the next train home for the funeral. Then he headed back to the camps.

One day during his quiet time, an inner voice seemed to tell him, "Today you are going to get the visa for Yugoslavia." He could hardly believe it. In the time he'd been working in the camps, he'd nearly forgotten the visa applications he'd filed for several communist countries.

When the mail arrived later that morning, Andrew received a letter from the Yugoslavian embassy at The Hague. *This is the word I've been waiting for,* he thought as he ripped the envelope open and began to read a letter saying the Yugoslavian government regretted to inform him that his application for a visa had been denied.

What? He'd been so sure about what he'd heard. The message had been that he would get his visa that very day. Did that mean he should go right away and make another application at the Yugoslavian consulate in Berlin? Andrew ran to his room, grabbed a set of photographs, and hurried to the tramway. An hour later, he sat in the Yugoslavian consulate filling out yet another set of forms. He stopped at the line marked

"Occupation." Always before he'd written "missionary." In Glasgow, he had been taught to be open and transparent with everyone.

"Lord," he prayed, "what else could I put here?" Then he recalled Jesus' words: "Go ye, and teach all nations." That was it! He wrote "Teacher" on his application and handed it in.

"Have a seat over there, sir," an official told him, "I will examine your papers now." Twenty minutes later, he came back smiling and wished Andrew a pleasant journey to his country.

Andrew was so excited he had to tell someone. Since his family didn't have a phone he placed a long-distance call to Amsterdam.

Mr. Whetstra answered. "I thought you were in Berlin, Andrew?"

"I am. But I had to tell you my good news, Mr. Whetstra. I have in my hand two pieces of paper. One is a letter from the Yugoslavian consulate turning down my request for a visa. And the other is a passport, stamped with a visa by the Yugoslav people here. I've got it, Mr. Whetstra! I'm going behind the Iron Curtain as a missionary!"

"Then you'd better come home for your keys, Andrew?"

"I'm sorry, Mr. Whetstra, this is a bad connection. I thought you said *keys.*"

"I did. To your Volkswagen. We've talked it over and there's no un-talking us. Mrs. Whetstra and I decided months ago that if you got your visa, you would also get our automobile."

Andrew was overwhelmed. "You need the car for your business."

"Our business? Andrew, you are on the King's business! We've prayed about this, and these are our orders."

It was almost too wonderful to believe.

Andrew spent the next few days planning his trip and searching all over Amsterdam for any Christian printed material he could find in the Yugoslav languages. Then he carefully went over his car looking for places to conceal what he had found. He wondered how God was going to supply the money he would need for the trip. He also drove his new car to Amersfoort, imagining the expression on Mr. de Graaf's face.

It turned out Mr. de Graaf wasn't a bit surprised. "Yes," he nodded, "I thought you'd have it by now." Then he pulled an envelope out of his pocket and handed it to Andrew. "God told us that you will be needing an additional sum of money these next two months. And here it is."

Andrew didn't even open the envelope to see how much money was inside. He was more convinced than ever that God could and would provide everything he was going to need for his trip.

9

GOD MAKES SEEING EYES BLIND

Andrew stopped his car on the far side of a small village in Austria. Just ahead of him was the Yugoslavian border. In every corner of his Volkswagen, Andrew had crammed Bibles, portions of the Scriptures, and tracts that he knew were considered illegal "foreign propaganda." If such property were discovered by the border guards, the person carrying it would be in serious trouble.

So, for the first time, Andrew prayed what he called The Prayer of God's Smuggler: "Lord, in my luggage I have Scripture that I want to take to your children across this border. When you were on earth, you made blind eyes see. Now, I pray, make seeing eyes blind. Do not let the guards see those things that you do not want them to see."

Then Andrew started the engine and drove up to the border. Two guards jumped up and came out of their guardhouse. They seemed startled to see him.

Just a few formalities, they assured Andrew. He would soon be able to drive on. The first guard began looking through his tent and sleeping bag, where Andrew had hidden boxes of tracts.

"Do you have anything to declare?" the guard asked.

"My money, a wristwatch, and a camera," Andrew answered.

The second guard asked Andrew to take out one of his suitcases and open it. The guard lifted a stack of shirts. That left, in plain sight, a stack of Christian booklets—in two different Yugoslavian languages.

Andrew turned and looked back at the first guard to say, "It seems dry for this time of year." He asked that guard about the local weather and then told him how the climate in Holland was always wet. While they chatted, Andrew wondered what the second guard was doing behind him. It would take a miracle for that guard to not see those tracts!

Finally, Andrew couldn't stand it any longer. He turned back and found the second guard watching him and listening to the conversation. He wasn't even looking at the suitcase.

"Well, do you have anything else to declare?" the guard asked.

"Only small things." The Bibles and tracts were small.

"We won't bother with them," said the guard. Andrew closed his suitcase, the guard gave back his passport, and he drove into Yugoslavia.

In the Yugoslavian city of Zagreb, Andrew hoped to find a man named Jamil. The Dutch Bible Society had supplied his name and address. Jamil had ordered Bibles from them in the past. But the last time had been more than ten years earlier. Andrew knew that Jamil probably no longer lived at the address he had been given. But, having no other lead, he had written a letter telling Jamil that a Dutchman might visit his country in March.

Andrew did not know until later that the letter had been delivered to Jamil's old apartment house. The man who lived there now did not know Jamil, so he sent the letter back to the post office. The letter sat there for two weeks while postal workers located Jamil's new address. On the morning that Andrew drove into Zagreb, it was delivered to Jamil. He read the letter and was puzzled. Who was this mysterious Dutchman? What should he do?

Jamil took a tram to his old address. Then he stood in front of the building, wondering, *What else should I do?* He saw a blue Volkswagen with Dutch license plates pulling up in front of the building! A young man stepped out of the car only two feet away. Jamil grabbed Andrew's hands and welcomed him to Yugoslavia.

Jamil found a translator for Andrew—an engineering student named Nikola. With Nikola as his guide, Andrew set out to bring greetings to the Christians in that country.

His visa allowed him to stay in Yugoslavia for fifty days. In those fifty days, Andrew spoke at more than eighty meetings! In the northern part of the country, he could preach openly. In the south, he had to be more secretive. But everywhere he went, the Christians were thrilled to find out that other Christians cared about them—that they were not alone. They treasured the Bibles and tracts that Andrew brought.

In one of the smallest churches, Andrew had his first serious trouble with the police. The church was the *Molitven Dom*—the "prayer house." It was really just a room in the house of its only member, a woman named Anna. But when the word got around, a large crowd came to hear Andrew speak. Many came out of curiosity, never having met someone from another country.

Andrew and Nikola taught the people a hymn. Then Andrew told the story of Jesus, knowing that many there had never heard it. They began a second hymn. Suddenly, someone pounded on the door.

Anna answered, and two policemen in uniform stepped into the room. The crowd fell silent as the policemen took out notebooks and began to write down the names of the people there. Then they asked questions about Andrew and Nikola.

After the police left, some of the Christians left as well. No one wanted to sing hymns after that. But at the end of the service, Andrew asked if anyone wanted to be a follower of Jesus, and several people raised their hands.

"You've seen tonight what following Christ might mean," Andrew warned. "Are you sure you want to become his people?" They nodded.

After Andrew left Yugoslavia, the police closed Anna's *Molitven Dom.* They called Nikola to court and questioned him. He was reprimanded and had to pay a fine. Another man who had helped them find Anna's little church was deported from the country.

Most roads in Yugoslavia were not paved. The bumps were rough, and terrible dust sifted in even with the car windows rolled up. Andrew didn't know what damage was being done to the little Volkswagen. So each morning, he and Nikola prayed, "Lord, we don't have the time or the money for repairs. Please keep this car running."

In 1957 cars and trucks were uncommon in that part of the world. So when two vehicles passed each other, the drivers usually stopped to share information about road conditions and where gasoline could be found.

One morning Andrew and Nikola stopped to talk to the driver of a truck. "I think I know who you are," he told them. "You're the Dutch missionary who is to preach in Terna tonight."

"That's right," Andrew answered.

"And this is the Miracle Car? The car that you pray for each morning?" Andrew and Nikola laughed and nodded yes.

The truck driver was a mechanic. He asked if he could look at the VW's engine. When he opened the hood, he stared at the motor.

"Brother Andrew," he said, "Look at the air filter! The sparks! The carburetor! It is mechanically impossible for this car to run!"

Andrew and Nikola followed the man to Terna. While they preached that night, the mechanic took the engine apart, cleaned and fixed it, and changed the oil. The next morning, Andrew and Nikola drove away in a car that drove like new.

Their last stop in Yugoslavia was Belgrade. Andrew preached in a church so crowded that someone took a door off the hinges so the people in the choir room could hear. As usual, at the end of the service, Andrew asked for those people who wanted to give their lives to Jesus to raise their hands. Everyone in the room responded.

Andrew explained how serious such a decision could be and made a second appeal. This time he asked them to stand. Everyone stood.

Andrew began to explain about their need for prayer and Bible study. As long as he talked about prayer, everyone was listening. But when he began to talk about Bible study, he saw a change in their faces.

The pastor explained. Prayer they could do. But of all the people in the room, only seven had Bibles. Only seven Bibles for people to read and learn about the God so many had just promised to follow.

That night, Andrew made a promise to God. He would find more Bibles—somehow, somewhere—and he would keep bringing them to God's children behind the Iron Curtain.

10

ANDREW PRAYS FOR A WIFE

One night in Yugoslavia, Andrew prayed, "Lord, in a year I'll be thirty. So I'm going to ask for something. I ask you tonight for a wife."

He wrote on the back cover of his Bible: "April 12, 1957. Nosaki. Prayed for a wife."

Leaving Yugoslavia and driving back across Europe, Andrew realized he dreaded going home to his lonely room. At a rest stop in Germany, he pulled out his Bible and read what he had written on the back cover. Andrew decided to pray again for a wife before going home to Witte.

For the next few weeks, he stayed busy, visiting friends, writing articles, and speaking at churches.

In July he prayed again: "Lord, I've got to pray just one more time about this bachelor life. . . . It isn't that I don't thank you for this room above the tool shed. But, dear God, it is not a home. A home has a wife and children. Some people are suited for the lonely walk, Lord. But not me.

"Lord, I have prayed two times for a wife. Perhaps you will refuse me a third time too. If you do, I shall never again bring up the question." Then Andrew wrote in the back of his Bible: "Prayed for wife. Third time. Witte. July 7, 1957."

One day in September, while praying about other things, Andrew suddenly thought of Corrie van Dam, the beautiful blonde girl who had worked with him at the chocolate factory. *Could this thought be from God?* he wondered.

Four years had passed since Andrew left Ringer's for school in England. Corrie had begun nursing school about the same time. She could be out of school by now—maybe even married!

That very morning, Andrew hopped in his car and drove to the van Dam house in Alkmaar. But it looked like no one lived there anymore. So he went by the chocolate factory to ask Mr. Ringer about Corrie. His old boss grinned and told Andrew he hadn't heard that Corrie had married. And he didn't know where she lived. Perhaps Andrew could contact Saint Elizabeth's Hospital, where Corrie had gotten her nurse's training.

Andrew finally learned Corrie's father was ill, and she was taking care of him. They had moved from their home to an apartment so Mr. van Dam wouldn't have to climb stairs.

It was several days before Andrew could get back to Alkmaar. When he knocked on the van Dams' door, Corrie answered.

"I've come to see your father," Andrew told her. He visited Mr. van Dam twice a week, talking to Corrie each time by the front door. Between visits, he imagined proposing. *Please marry me, Corrie. I'll be gone much of the time, and I won't be able to give you an address where you can write. We'll be in missionary work, but you'll never be able to talk about the people we're working with. If I don't come back, you'll probably never know what happened. Add to that no regular income and a room over a tool shed to call home.* Andrew couldn't picture Corrie saying yes to such a proposal.

In October he got his visa to travel to Hungary, and Andrew finally decided how he would propose. He would ask her to marry him before he left on the trip but urge her not to answer until he got back. She could think about it while he was gone, and it would give her an opportunity to see what such a life would be like.

Having made his decision, he drove immediately to Alkmaar. When he knocked on the van

Dam's door, no one answered at first. Then Corrie finally opened the door. Andrew looked at her face and knew immediately what was wrong.

"Your father?" he asked.

"He died half an hour ago," she replied.

It was hardly the right time to propose. Except for the funeral, Andrew didn't see Corrie again for three weeks. Then, right before he left for Hungary, he asked Corrie to go for a drive with him.

"Corrie," he told her, "I want you to marry me. But don't say yes or no until I tell you how hard it will be." Then he described what their lives would be like. "You'd be crazy to say yes, Corrie," he concluded. "But I do so want you to!"

Corrie promised to give him her answer when he returned from Hungary.

Andrew left for Hungary with every Hungarian-language Bible he had been able to buy or beg—that was not very many—and boxes full of Christian booklets. In the refugee camps, he had heard such fearful stories about Hungary that he didn't know what to expect.

At the border, God again made seeing eyes blind. But a few minutes later, Andrew got a taste of how fearful Hungary could be when he pulled off the road beside the Danube River to fix his lunch. He took out his camp-type stove and began heating up a can of peas and carrots for lunch. He heard a roar and saw a speedboat coming toward him across the river. Two soldiers in uniform jumped from the boat. One held a machine gun, pointed at Andrew, while the other searched his car.

"Lord," Andrew prayed, "don't let me give in to fear." He continued to stir the peas and carrots and began to talk.

"It certainly is nice to have you drop in this way." Andrew spoke in Dutch, knowing the soldiers probably did not understand. "As you can see, I am preparing to eat." He got out some extra plates and gestured with them. "Care to join me?'"

The man with the machine gun shook his head.

Andrew could hear the rustling sound of the other soldier looking through the car. How could he not see the boxes of Bibles and tracts?

Andrew spooned vegetables onto his plate, bowed his head, folded his hands, and said a blessing. The soldiers got very quiet. When he finished, the car door slammed shut, and the man searching his car marched over. For a moment both soldiers stared at Andrew. Then they wheeled about, ran to their boat, and sped away.

In Budapest, the Hungarian capital, Andrew met Professor B, who agreed to be his interpreter. He learned that about a third of the pastors in Hungary had been thrown in prison following the revolt. The remaining pastors were required to have a government permit and renew those permits every two months. He met a pastor who was now painting lampshades. His permit had been denied, and the government didn't tell him why. He wasn't even allowed to attend his own church.

Professor B asked Andrew to speak at a wedding. He was to congratulate the bride and groom, then preach his best sermon. Except for weddings and funerals, people were afraid to attend church. So they used those occasions to preach!

Andrew explained how in other countries, he had been able to bring greetings from Holland and from the Lord. Professor B loved that idea. He found several churches for Andrew to greet.

Their first stop was at one of the largest churches in town. At the end of the service, they announced that a meeting would be held in a certain location the next night. People lined up on the sidewalks outside the churches, just to hear the Dutch preacher. And each night, Professor B and his friends would look over the crowd to see if the secret police were present. One night they were. Professor B and Andrew were taken into a back room, questioned, and given a summons to the police station the next morning.

Professor B, Andrew, and five pastors gathered to pray. They prayed like many Christians have prayed over the years—in secret, in trouble, asking God to save them from those who would hurt or imprison them. At 11:35 P.M. that night, all seven of them stopped praying. They knew that God had answered their prayers. They didn't know how, but they were certain everything would be all right the next day.

Waiting at police headquarters the next morning, Professor B explained that the chief hated churches, but his deputy chairman was more lenient. Unfortunately, they were scheduled to see the chief. After waiting almost three hours, however, they were taken to the deputy's office.

The chief had become ill during the night. Andrew was sure it had happened about 11:35 P.M.

The deputy merely informed them that they could not hold any more meetings in Budapest. So Professor B contacted pastors from churches that Andrew could greet in eastern Hungary.

When his time was up in Hungary, Andrew anxiously headed for home. He didn't even stop in Witte. He drove directly for Haarlem to meet Corrie as she walked out of the hospital after work.

"I love you, Corrie," Andrew told her. "I love you whether the answer is yes or no."

"Oh, Andrew," she replied. "I love you too. That's just the trouble. I'm going to worry about you and miss you and pray for you no matter what. So wouldn't it be better if I were a worried wife than just a cranky friend?"

Corrie and Andrew were married in Alkmaar on June 27, 1958.

11

THE MINISTRY GROWS STRONG

A few months later, Amdrew and Corrie were working as volunteers in the refugee camps in Germany when he decided to try to take a precious load of Bibles into Yugoslavia. Once again he applied for and received the necessary visas from the Yugoslav consulate in Berlin. Corrie would travel with him—their first time together behind the Iron Curtain.

The border guards hardly even glanced at the luggage. They'd taken Andrew and Corrie for newlyweds and let them know where they should go and what they should see while honeymooning in their beautiful country. Andrew realized that a man and a woman traveling together aroused far less suspicion than a man traveling alone.

Together they traveled from one church to another. Whenever they presented a Bible to a congregation, the people could hardly believe their good fortune. The women hugged and kissed Corrie while the men pounded Andrew on the back.

The first six days in Yugoslavia were a complete success. But on the evening of the seventh day, while Andrew and Corrie were eating dinner with friends, the police came. "Don't finish your meal. Don't talk." ordered the officers. "Just come with us." The police knew all about Andrew's previous trip to Yugoslavia and informed him that he and his wife would have to leave the country immediately. Their visas had been canceled.

"Andrew, I was scared stiff!" Corrie kept saying after they left Yugoslavia and were driving across Austria toward Germany. "And those men were being polite about it."

Andrew was concerned about being kicked out of Yugoslavia, but he was even more concerned about Corrie's health. She was throwing up every day. He wanted to get her home to see a doctor as fast as he could.

During a stopover in Berlin, he got the exciting word that two more communist countries—Romania and Bulgaria—were ready to grant him visas if he would just come by their consulates.

But that would have to wait as Andrew hurried his wife back to Witte and summoned a doctor.

"Your wife is fine," the doctor told him. "But for heaven's sake, stop dragging that girl all over Europe and let her get some rest. And congratulations! You're going to be a father."

Within a couple of months, Corrie was doing so much better that Andrew began to think about Bulgaria and Romania. Corrie still hadn't gotten over the shock of their arrest in Yugoslavia.

Just the same, when the shipment of Bulgarian and Romanian Bibles from a British Bible society arrived, she helped Andrew stow them away in the nooks and crannies of the little Volkswagen. "A bargain's a bargain," she said. "After all, I signed on as the wife of a missionary."

When the day came for him to leave, Corrie made Andrew promise to be careful. "If you get arrested in one of those countries, I might never hear from you again. We want you back, Andrew. Your baby and I want you back."

The only reasonable way to drive to Bulgaria was through Yugoslavia, where he'd recently been expelled. Figuring the government was too disorganized to have informed their consulate in Berlin, Andrew applied for and received another visa. The guards at the border crossing barely looked at his passport. By his calculations, he would have four days before his arrival would be reported to the authorities in the capital of Belgrade—more than enough time to look up some old friends, visit a few churches, and be across the country's eastern border into Bulgaria.

But he was making so many valuable contacts and still had more people to see after the fourth day that Andrew decided he would risk another twenty-four hours. That night there was a loud knock on his hotel room door. The police had found him and demanded to know why he'd come back to Yugoslavia. They were not satisfied when he explained he was really just passing through on his way to Bulgaria.

They ordered him not to make any further contacts with Yugoslav citizens and gave him twenty-four hours to exit the country at the same place he came in. He pointed out that he was only fifty miles from the Bulgarian border and could get out of the country quicker if he went on. But they insisted he go back. This meant that he would have to drive down the length of Italy, take a ferry to Greece, and drive into Bulgaria from the opposite direction—fifteen hundred miles of added driving and expense.

Andrew felt discouraged until something so incredible happened that he was convinced God had special plans and was taking care of every detail of his trip. On his final night in Yugoslavia, the extra night that got him kicked out of the country, Andrew had met a man who said his closest friend lived in the Bulgarian city of Sofia. "Petroff is one of the saints of the church," the man said. "Will you go see him?"

Andrew was delighted to find a contact in Bulgaria. He memorized Petroff's address so he would have nothing in writing if he got in trouble with authorities. But once he reached Sofia, he wondered how he was going to find Petroff's place in such a large city. His Yugoslav friend had warned him Petroff would be in danger if a foreigner asked for his address.

Andrew checked into a hotel. Then he asked the clerk where he could purchase a map of the city. The clerk said they were out and suggested a bookstore around the corner. Learning the bookstore was also sold out, Andrew returned to the hotel clerk. "Are you sure there are no maps at all?" he asked. The man looked at him suspiciously and asked, "Why do you need a map?"

"Oh," Andrew assured him, "I don't speak Bulgarian. I just want to make sure I don't get lost."

That seemed to satisfy the clerk. "All we have is this little map," he responded, pointing to a small, hand-drawn street plan under the glass on his desk. Andrew could see that it contained only the major streets of the city. He knew it would do him no good, but he bent over the map anyway and pretended to be interested. Indeed, whoever drew the crude map had written in the names of only a handful of the main streets ... with one exception. There was a single, tiny street just a few blocks from the hotel that had a name written on it. And that was the very street Andrew was looking for! Not another small street on the entire map had been given a name—just that one. Andrew knew that his trip had been prepared long before.

The next morning Andrew walked out of the hotel and soon reached the street where Petroff lived. Now all he had to do was find the right number. As he walked along the sidewalk, he noticed a man approaching from the opposite direction. They came together at the very number Andrew was looking for—a large apartment building—and both turned up the walkway at the same time. As they neared the front door of the building, Andrew glanced at the stranger. In that instant, Andrew said, "Our spirits recognized each other."

They marched side-by-side up the stairs without a word. When the stranger reached his apartment, he took out a key and opened the door. Andrew walked right in, and the man closed the door behind them. "I am Andrew from Holland," the Dutchman said in English.

"And I," said the stranger, "am Petroff."

The two men embraced as Andrew offered greetings from Petroff's friend in Yugoslavia. Then Petroff introduced Andrew to his wife, and the three of them got down on their knees and thanked God for bringing them together.

"I've heard," Andrew said after they had talked a while, "that both Bulgaria and Romania are desperately in need of Bibles. Is that so?"

In answer, Petroff led him over to his desk. There Andrew saw an ancient typewriter and a Bible open to the book of Exodus. Petroff explained that just three weeks before, he'd found a Bible that was being sold cheap—for just one month's pension—because Genesis, Exodus, and Revelation had been cut out. He was typing up the missing pages from his own Bible and expected to finish in another four weeks or so.

"What will you do with the second Bible?"

"Give it away," he replied.

"To a little church," his wife added, "where there's no Bible."

"There are many such churches in this country," Petroff said when he saw Andrew's look of surprise. "You'll find the same in Romania and Russia. In the old days only the priests had Bibles because the common people couldn't read. Since communism, it's been impossible to buy them."

Andrew could hardly wait to show Petroff the treasure he had in his car. That evening he drove his car up to the apartment building, checked to make sure the street was empty, and hurried inside with the first of many cartons of Bibles he would deliver to this man over the years. "What's that?" Petroff asked as Andrew set the box on their one little table. Andrew lifted the lid and took out a Bulgarian Bible. He placed it in Petroff's trembling hands and gave another to his wife.

"And in the box?" Petroff wanted to know.

"More Bibles. And still more outside."

Petroff closed his eyes. His lips began to quiver, and tears of joy began to roll down his face and drop onto the book in his hands.

Andrew and Petroff set out the next day on a trip around Bulgaria, delivering Bibles to churches that had none. Many met secretly in homes or apartments, worshiping quietly without any music or hymns so they would not be heard and reported to the authorities by their neighbors.

Everywhere they went, Andrew brought greetings from Holland and from the Lord. And at every church, the people were so excited to receive a new Bible that they would suggest other churches he must visit.

"We've been waiting years for encouragement like this," the Bulgarian Christians told him. But Andrew was soon out of Bibles and knew it was time to go on to Romania.

"I wish I were ten people," he told his new Bulgarian friends. "I wish I could split myself into a dozen parts and answer every call that comes. Someday I am going to find the way to do it."

12

A LETTER TO HANS

Names and faces were different in Romania, but the stories were much the same as in Bulgaria. Border crossing guards carefully removed and inspected every item in the five cars in line ahead of Andrew, spending at least a half hour per vehicle. Any close inspection of his VW would reveal the boxes of Romanian Bibles stashed under his things. So while the guards pulled out seats of the car in front of him, Andrew prayed for another miracle. He actually placed some of his Bibles in plain sight on the seat, and told God, "No amount of cleverness on my part can get me through, Lord. I'm depending completely on you."

When it was his turn, Andrew gave the officer his travel papers, and started to get out. But the man took one look at the passport, wrote something down, shoved the papers back through the open window, and waved Andrew on. In less than thirty seconds! God was surely at work!

Police control was tight throughout Romania. Some church leaders were so frightened they didn't want to be seen talking to Andrew. They refused to take Bibles for fear that they might be questioned or arrested. But to some discouraged Christians, Andrew's greetings from "your Christian brothers in Holland" provided much-needed encouragement. He promised them he would tell others back home about their courage and their needs. After years of isolation and suffering, hearing they were not alone and that others were praying for them was enough to give many Romania Christians the hope required to maintain their faith.

The days passed quickly, and Andrew soon ran out of Bibles. He longed to stay and make more contacts, but Corrie's time was getting shorter. He wanted to be home before the baby's birth.

And he was. Andrew and Corrie's first son arrived on June 4, 1959. Joppie was born at home with Andrew watching, just as his father had been for the birth of Andrew and his siblings.

As little Joppie grew, so did Andrew's ministry. The following year Andrew revisited every country he could get back into, several more than once. With that growth came new challenges.

Because he continued to write articles and speak about his work, correspondence piled up in his absence. It often took him weeks to catch up.

An even bigger problem was the attention he was receiving from his articles and speaking engagements. If he kept using his real name, he worried that it might limit his freedom to come and go across borders safely. He decided to stop using his full name and to go by "Brother Andrew." That was the name he was called behind the Iron Curtain. Many Christians there had stopped using last names. He also rented a post office box number in another town, where people could send inquiries about his work. These were small precautions. He knew anyone who really wanted to learn his identity could do so.

The biggest problem with his expanding work was the added time away from home. Traveling had posed no problem for him as a bachelor, but now he had a wife and baby who needed him.

Mr. Ringer let him know that there was always a management job for him at the chocolate factory, and a church in the capital city invited him to become its pastor. But each time he received a tempting offer, a letter with no return address would arrive. Those letters, postmarked somewhere in Eastern Europe, spoke of new troubles or serious needs facing Christian brothers and sisters there. Then Andrew would pack his bags, load up his little car with Bibles, and set out again to help encourage and strengthen that which remained of the church in some communist land.

God continued to protect Andrew in amazing ways. And even though he didn't talk about the expense of his ministry, the Lord also provided for ministry and family needs with a steady flow of donations (most of them small) from people who read his articles and heard him speak.

There always seemed to be just enough to cover expenses, even the expense of two more children born in the next two years—first Mark Peter and then Paul Denis—and the purchase of a home.

Clearly Andrew needed help with the work if he was going to fulfill his family responsibilities. "If God wants us to expand the work, he certainly will have prepared the people," Andrew said to Corrie one night. "But how do I find them?"

"Try prayer," his wife told him.

Andrew laughed. Of course, Corrie was right. They prayed right then. Immediately, Andrew thought of a name. Hans Gruber was a giant of a Dutchman—six feet, seven inches tall. Andrew had worked with him in the refugee camps.

The next day Andrew wrote Hans, asking if he would consider working as a missionary to the communist world. If he accepted, Andrew said, his first trip would be to the Soviet Union, which had just relaxed travel restrictions. Foreigners would now be allowed to visit without being escorted by an official Intourist guide.

Hans accepted Andrew's offer. Since the sixth grade (the last year of school he attended), he had felt a strange sensation every time he looked at a map of Russia—as if a voice kept telling him, *Someday you will work for me in that land.* "Ever since then," Hans wrote, "I've studied Russian so I would be ready when the time came."

The time had come. Andrew and his new partner immediately began preparing for their first trip together into the motherland of communism—Soviet Russia. The old blue Volkswagen had seen better days. And there was no way for Hans to cram himself into the tiny car. The men purchased an Opel station wagon. Not only did it provide enough room to carry a good many more Bibles, but also it was big enough to sleep in. They could save money on hotel bills.

Andrew and Hans stopped in Berlin on their way, and the friends they stayed with were so excited about the idea of smuggling Bibles into Russia that they wanted to donate some of the Russian Bibles their church had. Andrew thought the car was full enough already. "But of course we'll take them," Hans agreed before turning to Andrew and grinning. "If we're going to get arrested for carrying in Bibles, we might as well get arrested for carrying in a lot of them."

They had squeezed those Bibles in when other friends arrived with a whole box of Ukranian Bibles. There was no more storage space left. Andrew looked at Hans, who grinned and told him, "You told me about leaving Bibles out in plain sight, so God can do the job and not you. I'll just carry these on my lap."

The Russian border guards at Brest seemed more interested in looking under the hood of the new Opel than searching the car. Then the soldiers simply stamped the necessary papers and wished Andrew and Hans well. They were in.

Andrew knew one man from the Moscow Protestant Church, so he and Hans went there to a Thursday evening prayer meeting. They didn't see Andrew's friend in the congregation, so they wandered around the crowded vestibule after the service praying silently that God would lead them to someone they could trust. Hans and Andrew felt led to the same man—a thin, balding gentleman in his forties who stood by himself along the wall.

Hans greeted the man in Russian and began to tell him who they were and where they were from. When he heard the word *Dutch*, the man burst out laughing. He said his parents were Germans who immigrated to Siberia, but his family still spoke their old language in their home. Then he began to tell Andrew and Hans an incredible story. This man belonged to a little church in Siberia, two thousand miles away, where one hundred fifty members worshiped every week without any Bible. One day in a dream, he had been told to go to Moscow, where he would find a Bible for his church. He had resisted the idea at first because everyone knew there were precious few Bibles in Moscow. But he'd finally decided to follow the directions in his dream.

The two Bible smugglers looked at each other in disbelief. Andrew nodded for Hans to tell the man the good news. "You were told to come westward for two thousand miles to get a Bible," Hans said. "We were told to go eastward two thousand miles carrying Bibles to churches in Russia. And here we are tonight, recognizing each other the instant we meet." With that, Hans handed the man a large Russian Bible. The Siberian man stood speechless for a few seconds. Then there were Russian bear hugs all around.

As in all the countries they visited, Andrew and Hans ran out of Bibles long before they ran out of churches and people who needed them. No matter how many they were able to hide in a car, it never seemed to be enough.

Part of the problem was the size of each book. Russian, like other Slavic languages, is written in Cyrillic script instead of the smaller and simpler

Latin alphabet. So each Russian Bible took as much room as three or four Dutch or English versions.

On their way home through the Ukraine, Andrew and Hans distributed their one box of Ukrainian Bibles. At one of the churches, they met a Christian who showed them a pocket-sized Ukrainian Bible. Andrew marveled at the tiny yet crisp and readable type. Then and there a dream was born. They would find an organization willing to print Slavic-language Bibles in pocket-size editions. Then they could bring them into Russia by the thousands.

Three years later, that dream came true. To help make it happen, Andrew's organization printed its own edition. In the meantime, the trips to other countries continued, the work grew, and a young man named Rolf and his wife, Elena, joined Andrew's missionary team. Rolf went with him to Moscow, where they delivered 650 copies of the compact edition of the Russian Bible.

As the years passed and Andrew's ministry spread to more and more countries, his nonprofit organization, which he named Open Doors, added more missionaries and continued to look for new opportunities to encourage Christians who were being persecuted for their beliefs in Christ. For example, Andrew was able to take automobiles into communist countries as gifts from Western Christians to pastors who would never have been able to afford private transportation, enabling them to travel more freely and broaden their ministries. But the primary work of Open Doors continued to be the encouragement of Christian bothers and sisters in suffering churches. They took them Bibles, shared the love of God with them, and reminded them that they were not alone.

As new Open Doors missionaries did much of the traveling, Andrew did even more writing and speaking. He told Western Christians about the work of Open Doors and the incredible needs of fellow believers living in countries where being a Christian could mean persecution, imprisonment, and sometimes even torture and death.

He wrote a book telling about his calling. He recounted how he'd seen God work and described some of the inspiring Christians he'd met in communist countries. *God's Smuggler* became a best-seller. It sold millions of copies and drew attention to the needs of the suffering church around the world. The book also brought new interest and support for the work of Open Doors. Andrew broadened his dream to include new parts of the world, where he might follow the command God had given him years before: to "strengthen what remains and is about to die."

13

A BARGE FULL OF BIBLES

One day on a bus in Moscow, Andrew sat down next to a Chinese man who was wearing a cross on his lapel. Andrew introduced himself and learned his seatmate was the secretary of the Shanghai YMCA. Andrew could hardly believe his ears. A Young Men's Christian Association in communist China? The man gave Andrew his business card and invited him to visit.

That meeting initiated a new dream in Andrew's heart. He would reach out to the Christians in China. Andrew wondered how many there were. Many missionaries had gone to China before the communist revolution. What had become of those mission churches? Were their members being persecuted for their faith? Did they need Bibles too?

Andrew went on a speaking tour to California, and from there, he flew to Taiwan to talk to people about how to get into Mainland China. From Taiwan he flew to Hong Kong. The man sitting next to him on the plane explained that the authorities would never let him into China, because he was coming from Taiwan. And he would certainly not be admitted with a U.S. stamp on his passport.

Andrew checked in at the Hong Kong YMCA and was told again and again that the Chinese would never allow him to enter the country with stamps from Taiwan and the U.S. on his passport.

Finally Andrew went to the Dutch consulate and explained that he was a missionary wishing to travel to Mainland China. The consul checked his passport and told him it would be "impossible" for him to get into the country. His current passport would keep him out, and a new passport could not be issued.

For Andrew that meant it was up to God to work out the details.

The next morning he went to the Chinese Travel Service, the government agency handling visas. One of the first questions the official asked was, "Have you ever been to the United States or to Taiwan?"

"I have just come from Taiwan. And before that I was in the U.S."

"Then you cannot possibly enter China," the official explained. "Those countries are our enemies."

Andrew filled out the forms anyway, and for the next three days, he fasted and prayed. On the third day, he got his visa.

A train took Andrew from Hong Kong to the border of communist China. There he was one of only six people who walked, single file, across the railroad bridge and into China.

The guard who checked his suitcase at the border was a young woman. Andrew opened his suitcase. The guard glanced at the Bibles, clear for anyone to see. Then she passed him on. Andrew wondered, *Had she ever seen a Bible? Perhaps she didn't know what it was.*

Getting into the country had seemed like a miracle. Yet once there, Andrew did not have one positive encounter with a Christian. He found a Bible store that had many Bibles but no customers. He visited a seminary that taught its students to hate Americans and didn't seem to teach them to love Jesus. He was unable to persuade even one person to take one of the Bibles he had brought with him. The only church he was able to find was attended by a handful of very elderly people. Andrew went home discouraged but still concerned about the church in China.

Then in 1970 Andrew met with a man named Brother David, who also wanted to take Bibles into China. David worked for a broadcasting company that beamed daily radio programs into China, telling the good news of Jesus. He was praying for the opportunity to take ten million Bibles into China.

He and Andrew came up with an exciting new way to get Bibles safely in the hands of Chinese Christians. At that time the Chinese people often carried a small book around with them. Mao's Little Red Book is a collection of the sayings of Chairman Mao Tse-tung, the first communist ruler of China. Why not print a New Testament, Andrew and David thought, in the same size, shape, and color and call it the Jesus Red Book? Since it looked just like Mao's book, people could carry it in public without arousing suspicion.

That day Andrew placed an order for twenty-five thousand copies of the Jesus Red Book. And over the next few months, David found ways to get them into China. He located Chinese Christians living in other countries and asked them to take some Jesus Red Books with them whenever they went home for a visit. He searched out little-known mountain passes and little-used border crossings into the country, through which Bibles could be taken by traders. Before long, all twenty-five thousand Bibles made their way over the border.

David and Andrew kept dreaming of the day those ten million Bibles would go into China. And those dreams eventually resulted in their most daring operation yet. After more than a year of planning and prayer, they smuggled one million Bibles into China on a single night. "Project Pearl" got its name because so many Chinese Christians were willing to risk their lives for the pearls of God's Word.

One million Bibles weighed too much to be flown in, but they could be taken in by boat. David and Andrew began to search for a beach. On the southern coast of China, near the city of Swatow, they discovered a small beach village where most of the people were Christians. Those Christians were willing to risk their lives to bring Bibles into their country.

Now the question was what type of boat to use for the mission. A barge pulled by a tugboat is a common sight along the coast of China. They would make a good cover. But the tugboat and barge would need special modifications.

Tugboats usually sleep only four or five men. They needed one that could sleep twenty men. They found a tug in Singapore that had been built but not finished. For about $480,000, they were able to customize it to fit their plan. A church in California agreed to cover most of the cost. They named the tugboat *Michael*.

Storing a million Bibles in the barge wasn't a problem. But getting them from barge to shore quickly required some ingenuity. They built a special barge that could take on water on one side and "sink" until its deck was below the surface and the cargo could float off. The barge they named *Gabriella*.

The tugboat, with Brother David aboard, weighed anchor and headed north along the coast of China. A radio message went out to the Christian leaders in China: "We are having a dinner party. Expecting so many people that we have arranged twenty-one teacups and cooked eighteen bowls of rice." That way the believers in China knew that the boats would arrive at 2100 hours— 9:00 P.M.—on June 18.

When the boats approached the coast, the sea was calm and the weather good. Darkness fell before they reached shore. David quickly flashed a bright light three times toward the beach. Three flashes answered back immediately. The Chinese Christians were ready.

The tugboat pulled *Gabriella* as close to land as possible. The crew on the barge began to submerge the deck. Three rubber powerboats were lowered into the water. And David, on one of those powerboats, made his way to shore to greet the people waiting there.

All 232 one-ton blocks of cargo, packaged in waterproof wrapping, floated free. And the three powerboats began towing the Bibles to shore.

On the beach, more than two thousand Chinese Christians formed a chain, some standing in water up to their necks. They passed the boxes along to the beach. There others cut the packages open and quickly moved them out of the open and into a nearby forest of trees.

Each one-ton package contained forty-eight boxes of Bibles. And each box was the right size so that two could be carried on a traditional bamboo rod over someone's shoulders. Or two boxes could be attached to a bicycle, using a rope.

Out of sight among the trees, the boxes were loaded onto waiting bicycles, cars, and trucks. As soon as they were full, these quickly drove away and headed for their destinations.

In less than two hours, all the boxes were off the barge. At 11:00 P.M. *Michael* and *Gabriella* headed back for international waters. By 1:00 A.M. the beach had been cleared and everyone was working under the cover of the trees. By 3:00 A.M. two-thirds of the shipment was on the road, moving inland.

That's when an army patrol descended on the hundreds of Christians still working in the trees and arrested many of them. They confiscated what they thought were all the remaining Bibles and tried to burn them. But books do not burn easily without fuel. In frustration, the soldiers threw the books into the sea.

Apparently some local fishermen had seen the activity on the beach and reported it to the authorities. But in the dark, the soldiers missed many of the boxes hidden in the trees. Later some of those were recovered by the Chinese Christians. Most of those arrested were released.

Other boxes were found by local people who took them home and hid them, hoping to make some money. Since they were not known to be Christians, their homes were not searched. And the church was able to buy them back later for ten cents each.

While the army was busy trying to burn the Bibles on the beach and arresting the people they had caught, they did not try to track any of the hundreds of bicycles, cars, and other vehicles, loaded with their precious cargo and driving away in all directions. Some of those Bibles traveled as far as three thousand miles to house churches all over China.

And the Bibles that were thrown into the sea? The next morning local fishermen recovered them, and for days black-covered books could be seen, drying on the rooftops of houses around Swatow.

14

ONE MILLION BIBLES FOR RUSSIA

The enormous success of Andrew's book, *God's Smuggler*, which is still in print and has sold more than ten million copies, proved an incredible blessing to Andrew and the ministry of Open Doors. Royalties from the book, along with many gifts contributed by readers, made it possible for Open Doors to purchase office and warehouse space, take on more missionaries, print or buy Bibles and Christian literature in a variety of languages, acquire more vehicles to transport Bibles, hire mechanics to customize and maintain them, and find the resources required to follow up on bigger dreams, such as Project Pearl.

But there was also a downside to the book and the fame it gave Andrew. He quickly realized he would not be able to return to many of the Iron Curtain countries for years without placing himself and his Christian contacts in great danger. That discouraged Andrew for a time.

Then he remembered how he and Corrie had prayed that their ministry team would grow from two to twelve to thousands. He realized he was being forced to find others to help carry on and expand the work in communist countries. Soon he'd recruited several new team members to follow up with his contacts and take encouragement to struggling believers.

But what did God have in mind for Andrew? He soon came to believe God was saying, "Yes, my church is suffering behind the Iron Curtain, but it is also suffering in other countries. You need to go to these places as well." Andrew began to travel to other trouble spots, where God's people were being persecuted for their faith—China, Africa, Central America, and the Middle East.

There was indeed much left to be done. But even as communism began to lose its grip on Eastern Europe during the 1980s, travel restrictions eased, and the hard lines of the Cold War gradually began to melt, Andrew's concern for his Christian brothers and sisters behind the old Iron Curtain continued. He knew many were still imprisoned and millions more still couldn't worship openly.

One day a Dutch businessman, a sort of behind-the-scenes diplomat, asked Andrew and Open Doors to organize an unofficial conference, where U.S. and Soviet leaders might come together as private citizens to openly discuss human rights issues. Andrew could hardly believe the opportunity. Here he was, a well-known Bible smuggler, asked to organize a meeting involving some of Russia's most important communist leaders.

Andrew didn't try to hide who he was or what he believed. In fact, he set up tables at the conference with free Bibles and Christian books—including *God's Smuggler*.

One day an officer of the KGB (the Russian secret police), who had been looking at the books on the table, asked Andrew to autograph a book on leadership.

"I'd be happy to," Andrew said. "And if you like," he added with a smile, "I could even sign my other book, *God's Smuggler.*"

"There is no need for that," the man said wryly. "We all have that book on our shelves in Moscow." It was required reading in the KGB.

Andrew's role at the conference was that of organizer and host, not an official participant. Yet throughout the conference, he couldn't stop thinking about two issues: The first was the continuing need for Russian Bibles. The second was a list he had of four hundred prisoners still being held in Soviet labor camps, prisons, and psychiatric institutions because of their beliefs.

Late in the conference, Andrew stood up and announced, "I would like to make a little speech." Everyone looked at him. While he'd spoken thousands of times to all kinds of audiences, he was feeling nervous, because he was going to offer to do something that had never been done before in the history of Russia. Bibles had been forbidden there even before the Bolshevik Revolution. Since then, almost all Bibles discovered by the authorities had been destroyed. But Andrew believed he was following God's instruction.

Saying a silent prayer, he began by telling the delegates what he'd been saying all over the world for years. No nation can be happy when its people are forced to live under a political or religious system that they have not freely chosen. "The same is true for the Soviet people," he said. "They can never be happy unless they have access to the alternative to communism—Jesus Christ." Everyone present knew he was a Bible smuggler, so he felt no hesitation about saying, "And I will continue to take Bibles to Russia in whatever way I can. I will do this until everyone in the churches has a Bible, everyone in the schools has a Bible, and the Bible is available in all bookshops so that people can simply walk in and buy the Word of God."

There was no turning back now.

"Therefore, as a beginning," he told them, "I am now offering a gift of one million Bibles to the Russian Orthodox Church in honor of their one thousandth birthday." Andrew went on to refer to the list of four hundred prisoners and urged the Soviet leaders at the conference to release them all. "As long as there is one person imprisoned in Russia for his faith in Jesus, I am not free! We will not stop when *most* of the prisoners have been released and Open Doors will not stop when a *great many* Bibles have been provided. We will continue until every prisoner has been released and everyone who wants a Bible has access to one."

It was quite a speech, and the response of the Russian delegation was surprisingly positive. At a press briefing at the end of the conference, one of Soviet President Mikhail Gorbachev's closest advisors, applauded Andrew's offer of one million Bibles. "I see no problem whatsoever," he said. "The Bible is not only a religious book but a book of great culture and moral value. I myself have a Bible at home."

A KGB general by the name of Andrei Grachev shook Andrew's hand as the delegates said goodbye. "You are welcome with your million Bibles, Andrew," he smiled. "But please don't do it all in one night like you did in China."

Andrew laughed. "Don't worry, Andrei. I won't. I won't."

The first shipment of one hundred thousand New Testaments was on its way to the Soviet Union by the following year. Andrew, who hadn't dared to go back to Russia for twenty years, went along to make the presentation in an official ceremony. Things were definitely changing.

Over the next few years not only did the old Soviet Union dissolve, but also the Berlin Wall came down, East and West Germany reunited, and communist regimes all over Eastern Europe came to an end. In many of those countries, Christians were at the center of the popular uprisings that toppled old, repressive governments and moved them toward democracy. Only God will ever know how many of those Christians kept their faith because of the encouragement and help they had received from the ministry of the Dutchman who became God's smuggler. However, the influence of communism still remains in places around the world. And wherever it reigns, Brother Andrew and Open Doors continue their work of encouraging persecuted Christians.

Today Brother Andrew has shifted much of his concern away from former communist countries in order to respond to the persecution of Christians in the Muslim world.

One day in the late 1970s, a Middle Eastern man approached Andrew at a conference and asked, "Brother Andrew, when are you coming to visit the churches in Iran?" Andrew hadn't realized there were any churches left in that Muslim country. But he quickly learned the truth.

In 1981 he and his partner Johan traveled to Iran to meet with and encourage the Christians there. It was a turbulent time in that nation's history. In November 1979, Iran had taken sixty-six hostages at the American embassy in Tehran and held them captive for more than four hundred days. They released the hostages in January 1981, a short time before Andrew and Johan arrived.

The Ayatollah Khomeini was at the height of his power. Iran was at war with Iraq. The national chaos seemed to be reflected in the condition of the airport. Hundreds of people waited hours for their luggage, sometimes fighting, yelling, and cursing in frustration. In the city, broken traffic lights caused accidents and traffic jams. Finally, they were able to reach their destination, a church housed in a small building. In a mosque across the square, a million Muslims prayed each Friday.

Andrew expected the Christians to complain about the difficult conditions. Instead, the church members said, "God has been good to us. Because of all the confusion, we have been able to use the same permit five times to print Bibles." And the social upheaval meant more Muslims were attending Christian churches, to hear about Jesus.

When Andrew came home from that trip, he decided that he would spend the rest of his life reaching out to the church in Muslim countries.

During the 1980s Andrew repeatedly visited war-torn Lebanon. He took Bibles to the prime minister, the president, and many of the generals fighting each other in that civil war.

One day on a flight to Beirut, Andrew noticed a man in the first-class section. He was wearing a turban, and bodyguards were protecting him. Andrew began to pray for this man and asked God for an opportunity to talk to him. Then he walked past the man to the bathroom. On the way back to his seat, he and the man struck up a conversation.

They talked for a few moments. The man was the Grand Mufti, the spiritual leader of all Sunni Muslims in Lebanon. Andrew gave him a copy of *God's Smuggler*, and the Grand Mufti invited Andrew to visit his office.

That's just what Andrew had wanted, a chance to talk more with this leader of Muslims. The Grand Mufti's palace was in the center of East Beirut. When he saw Andrew coming, the Grand Mufti greeted him by saying, "Andrew— that book you gave me. Every day after dinner, I have been reading it to my children."

They talked about their dreams of peace, and Andrew gave him a Bible. The Grand Mufti seemed so eager to talk about Jesus. Andrew hoped he would be able to talk with him again. But just six weeks later, the Grand Mufti and his bodyguards were killed by a car bomb.

Andrew once presented a Bible to Yassir Arafat and talked for some time about Jesus with the president of the Palestinian Liberation Organization (PLO). He learned there are many Christians among the Palestinians. When Andrew took time to speak with these fellow believers he says, "They poured out their pain to me—specifically the pain of not being recognized by the Western church as part of the body of Christ. They told me many Christians in the West are so obsessed with Israel and its place in biblical prophecy that they completely ignore the *church* in Israel, which is eighty-five percent Arab. Believers there feel lonely, abandoned, and betrayed."

One day Andrew was being interviewed on a Christian television show. He told the talk show host that communists and Muslims are not our enemies. "Well, Andrew," the host replied, "if these people are not our enemies, who is?"

"The devil," Andrew answered. "Never people."

He explained that as long as we think of a people as our enemies, we cannot love them.

Sharing the love of God is what Brother Andrew's ministry has always been about.

Today Andrew still lives with Corrie in Holland. They have five children and four grandchildren. Even though he is more than seventy years old, Brother Andrew has not slowed down much. He still travels a lot, pursuing his vision for encouraging and strengthening the church that remains in the Muslim world.

"I also believe God wants me to pray for Israel and strengthen our networks there," he says. "But at this time I think the best thing I can do for Israel is to win her enemies to Christ. So I continue to pray and travel throughout the Middle East and North Africa to share the gospel and build bridges."

When he is home, Brother Andrew walks the dikes and beaches of Holland every day. He eventually hopes to cover every dike and every beach in the country.

Walking the paths he ran on as a boy, Andrew does a lot of remembering. Gazing out over the seas, he feels the power and greatness of God. "And yet," he says, "there is still much to be done. Like the work of caring for the dikes, the work of spreading the gospel never seems to end." As long as he lives, he says, "I will continue to do my part, following wherever God leads." For the man known around the world as God's Smuggler, that's been the greatest adventure of his life.

Discover the hero in you with Today's Heroes books!

Written by Gregg & Deborah Shaw Lewis

Ben Carson
Softcover 0-310-70298-4

Colin Powell
Softcover 0-310-70299-2

David Robinson
Softcover 0-310-70297-6

Joni Eareckson Tada
Softcover 0-310-70300-X

Brother Andrew
Softcover 0-310-70313-1

Dave Dravecky
Softcover 0-310-70314-X

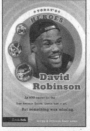

Available now at your local bookstore!

Zonder**kidz**™

Grand Rapids, MI 49530
www.zonderkidz.com